THE ECONOMICS OF DEFENSE

A Primer of American Mobilization

By RICHARD V. CLEMENCE, Ph. D.
*Associate Professor of Economics
Wellesley College*

THE STACKPOLE COMPANY
Harrisburg, Pennsylvania

Copyright 1953
By
The Telegraph Press

All Rights Reserved

L. C. Catalog Card Number: 53-5686

Printed in the U. S. A.

By

THE TELEGRAPH PRESS

Established 1831

Harrisburg, Pennsylvania

To a great teacher

LORA ELIZA OATLEY CLEMENCE

My Mother

PREFACE

I have called this book a primer not because it is small, but because I hope it can be understood by readers having no previous knowledge of the subject. The treatment is analytical, and is intended to provide insight into the course of events rather than a detailed description of it.

The use of the model technique largely accounts for the fact that I have been able to capture in my writing so much of the grace and elegance of a child's first reader. Extensive testing of earlier drafts has shown that the present style diminishes the difficulty of making continual shifts from the text to the diagrams and back again. The book is not designed for hasty reading, and whatever merits it may possess will be revealed only if it is worked through slowly, as it is meant to be.

Readers to whom the subject of defense mobilization is already familiar may be interested in the analytical technique and in possibilities of its further development. A number of different versions of this technique have been appearing recently; my own was originally derived some fifteen years ago from the Schumpeterian concept of the circular flow. The basic idea is, of course, nearly as old as economics itself, but little has ever been made of it as a pedagogical device.

R. V. C.

ACKNOWLEDGMENTS

This book has been more than two years in preparation, and I have missed few opportunities to obligate myself to my colleagues, friends, and casual acquaintances on account of it. My associates in the Department of Economics at Wellesley College have, as always, been both patient and helpful. Professors Lawrence Smith, Lucy W. Killough, Joseph T. Lambie, and Carolyn S. Solo, and Messrs. Nicholas A. Beadles and Norton T. Dodge are responsible for much of the improvement that took place between the first draft and the final version of the manuscript.

Among professional economists outside my own department, I am particularly indebted to Professor Francis S. Doody of the College of Business Administration, Boston University; Professor John Kenneth Galbraith and Mr. George Wright of Harvard University; and Dr. Arthur A. Bright, Director of Research at the Federal Reserve Bank of Boston.

For help with problems of communication I owe much to Dr. Gerald M. Clemence and members of the staff of the United States Naval Observatory, and to Mrs. James W. Thompson of the League of Women Voters in Wellesley.

Besides the persons I have named, a good many others have helped me substantially, and I regret my inability to make more specific acknowledgment to them.

Without the extraordinary cooperation of my wife, Eleanor Prescott Clemence, I could never have written this book or anything else.

R. V. C.

TABLE OF CONTENTS

CHAPTER 1. INTRODUCTION 1
    The Problem of Mobilization 1
    Mobilization and the Defense Economy 3
    Sources of Information 5
    The Model Technique 9

CHAPTER 2. THE PEACETIME ECONOMY ... 13
    The Model 15
    Production 15
    Consumption 17
    The Income Stream 18
    Saving and Investment 19
    The Price System 25
    Government 28

CHAPTER 3. THE WAR ECONOMY 31
    The Model 31
    The American Economy in Wartime 33
    Production and Consumption 35
    War Finance 37

CHAPTER 4. THE DEFENSE ECONOMY 39
    The Model 39
    The Economy During Mobilization 43
    Production 44
    Consumption 46
    Problems of Mobilization 47

CHAPTER 5. SHIFTING RESOURCES 51
Use of the Price System 51
Building Defense Capacity 52
Financing Mobilization 55
Mobilization and the Price System 57
Bottlenecks and Inflation 61

CHAPTER 6. INFLATION 63
The Meaning of Inflation 63
Causes of Inflation 64
The Mechanism of Inflation 66
The Cost-Price Spiral 72
Consequences of Inflation 79
Inflation in the Defense Economy 85

CHAPTER 7. INDIRECT CONTROLS 89
Money and Credit 90
Taxation 100
Inducements to Save 107
Production Goals 110

CHAPTER 8. DIRECT CONTROLS 113
Direct Controls and Voluntary Action 113
Price Controls 116
Wage Controls 122
Priorities and Allocations 124
Rationing 126
Government Ownership 132

CHAPTER 9. CONCLUSION 135

Chapter 1

INTRODUCTION

The American People are conducting a great experiment. For the first time in history we have undertaken to prepare ourselves for an all-out war before starting to fight one. Heretofore, we have managed, by a combination of skill and good fortune, to emerge victorious from one conflict after another despite our unpreparedness at the outset. In the present state of the world, however, it appears that for once at least the best way to prevent an all-out world war is to be thoroughly prepared to win one. This point of view, it is true, is not universally shared by the citizens of this country. Even aside from those who are pacifistic on moral and religious grounds, some people may hold honest doubts concerning the wisdom of our course of action. There is no way to prove that the minority is wrong, for no one knows beyond all question what choice between evils is to be preferred. Most Americans nevertheless have agreed that our best hope lies in a program of defense mobilization, giving visible evidence to the world that we and our allies are able and ready to resist immediately any move by an aggressor.

The Problem of Mobilization

The problem of mobilization for defense has two major aspects. To begin with, there is the whole question of physical possibilities. Has the United States, together with its allies, resources and manpower enough to build an impregnable defense against aggression? Unfortunately, this question simply cannot be answered in advance. Careful surveys of the potential strength of the nations of the world can be and have been made, but they merely prove in detail what everyone knows in general: Our chances are excellent, but cannot be guaranteed. The answer could hardly be anything else. Otherwise, we should either have been attacked, or threats to our security would have ceased long ago. It is only because there can be some doubt as to the outcome that the possibility of total war even exists. What we are doing, therefore, is all we can do: Mobilize our resources for defense, and hope that the display of strength will be sufficient to discourage attack.

The second aspect of mobilization is one about which a great deal can be done, and it is this aspect with which this book is primarily concerned. To prepare a democracy for all-out war is a very different matter from similarly preparing a totalitarian dictatorship. The American people have no intention of allowing themselves to be pushed around, either "for their own good" or for any other reason. Thoughtful people are naturally aware that some of their fellow citizens do not enjoy all the liberties they should, and that their disadvantages are no credit to this country. Nevertheless, in contrast to most great nations of the world, the people of the United States as a whole may justly pride themselves upon an extraordinary freedom of action, and their resentment at any real or fancied interference is something to be reckoned with very seriously. Mobilization in a dictatorship means telling people what to do, and making them do it. In the United States, we have to be shown why any given action is necessary, and without intelligent decision and action by individuals nothing can be accomplished.

Mobilization and the Defense Economy

Having decided to prepare ourselves thoroughly for defense, we should like to know how long the job will take. This question cannot be given a definite answer. One of the most exasperating features of the whole mobilization program is that it must be speeded up and slowed down in accordance with changing conditions. Every time the speed is increased, it appears that we must have been wasting vital time before. Whenever the speed is reduced, it similarly seems that we have been going unnecessarily fast, and that a lot of trouble and inconvenience has been suffered for nothing. At any given time, moreover, there is bound to be some difference of opinion as to the proper rate of mobilization to attempt. At every change of pace, many people thus tend to feel that a mistake is being made, while others are convinced that their own counsels should have prevailed sooner. In these circumstances, it is easy to see that although most people may agree that mobilization is necessary, few are likely to be altogether satisfied with the way things are going at any given time.

To see why the speed of mobilization cannot be determined once for all in advance, let us consider the possibilities:

All-out mobilization of the type to which we are accustomed in time of major wars is not feasible. This would require efforts and sacrifices far greater than a free people would tolerate except in the face of extreme and immediate danger. Furthermore, even if a tremendous war machine could be created, the question would then arise concerning what to do with it. Our enemies are already trying hard to foster the illusion that we are bent on aggression, and they would be only too glad to have tangible evidence to support their claims. A major war is exactly what defense mobilization is intended to avoid, and unless we were to attack some other nation, all-out mobilization would merely leave us with great armed forces to support indefinitely. It is often said, and doubtless with truth, that nothing would please our enemies more than to scare us into taxing our economic strength to build a vast war machine, after which they would make sure that we got no excuse to use it.

To all-out immediate mobilization there is hardly an opposite extreme short of doing nothing at all. Whether the slowest possible mobilization would take us a hundred years, or fifty, or some other number is merely playing with words. What we really want is a program that will give us sufficient armed strength to make it clear that we mean business, and that will prepare the whole nation for a rapid shift to an all-out war economy on short notice. The longer we can take in building up our capacity to produce war goods, the more strength we may ultimately achieve. New weapons may be designed and tested, and improved techniques of mass production may be developed as time goes on. Slow defense mobilization has the further advantage of interfering to the least possible extent with the private affairs of American citizens, requiring but a minimum of effort and sacrifice.

Beyond the bare essentials of first-line defensive power, it is expedient to proceed as slowly as we dare. But just how slowly is this? Obviously, nobody can be certain. The only feasible plan is to make a start, and then speed or slow the rate of mobilization as the danger of all-out war appears to be more—or less—imminent. It would be far better if we knew the intentions of our enemies and could plan accordingly, but this is quite out of the question. It is even within the range of possibilities that our enemies have no all-out war in mind to begin with, and that they are trying instead to keep us perpetually alarmed in the hope of creating the conditions for revolution or economic breakdown in this country. Certainly, good communist doctrine holds that capitalism is in the last stages of its career, and that it is due to collapse at any time now.

Our discussion of the speed of defense mobilization brings out a fact that is sometimes overlooked: Mobilization and the defense economy are not two stages of preparedness, but one. If conditions were quite different, we might be able to think of mobilization as a temporary affair. We could then say that mobilization is the process by which we build a defense economy, and that when the defense economy has been completed, mobilization will cease. This distinction between the process and the finished product, however, does not correspond to the facts. While the danger exists, we cannot stop improving our defenses. We must continue to build our defense economy during the foreseeable future, and though we may expect to be less unprepared as time goes on, we could regard ourselves as fully prepared only by denying all possibility of further progress.

Sources of Information

Although mobilization may be easier in a dictatorship

than in a democracy, it is not necessarily better done. When the people of a democracy agree on a major objective, and when they know what they are doing and why, their ability to get things done compares favorably with that of any totalitarian regime. In a democracy, moreover, the freedom of discussion that sometimes delays proper action frequently prevents improper action altogether. If errors are made, they are much more likely to be discovered and corrected when people not only select their leaders, but watch them closely and replace them if they choose. Given adequate information, the people of a democracy can make intelligent decisions and carry them out better than can any dictatorship.

In the United States there is no difficulty about getting information, and remarkably accurate information, too. So far as defense mobilization is concerned, most of us are likely to feel that there is too much information available rather than too little. Only a few specialists have time to read more than a small fraction even of the government publications on the subject, and other people are likely to wonder if they are reading the right things and enough of them. Everyone must naturally answer this question for himself in terms of the nature of his interests, and the time he has available. The following list may help the reader to reach his own particular answer:

1. Daily newspapers and news broadcasts report the day to day course of events as fast as the news is made. The chief trouble with the daily news is that there is too much of it, and we find it easier to get lost in the details than to get a clear picture of what is going on.

2. Weekly news magazines like *Time* and *Newsweek*

provide much of the desired perspective, and the Sunday editions of such newspapers as *The New York Times* carry excellent summaries of the week's developments.

3. Few of us have time for much besides the things already mentioned, and only those people who want to follow defense mobilization with extraordinary care have need of more. Trade journals carry discussions of the problems and prospects of particular industries, and these are read by those closely associated with the industries as a matter of course. Such weekly publications as *The United States News* and *Business Week* deal with broader questions, and have the special virtue of presenting clearly written summaries of government bulletins and documents, giving the reader a rather better idea of what they contain than he would get from attacking the originals.

4. Government publications like the *Economic Reports of the President,* the periodic reports of other government agencies, the *Survey of Current Business,* and the *Federal Reserve Bulletin* are not for most of us. Indeed, the busy taxpayer who encounters one of these for the first time may wonder if money is being well spent in distributing such masses of facts and figures. Since only a small fraction of the population makes much direct use of them, is the publication of such data worthwhile?

A similar question has occurred to a good many stockholders as they threw the annual report of some large corporation into the wastebasket. Despite the efforts of both public and private agencies to make their reports intelligible, these publications can scarcely qualify as popular literature. Their importance is measured, however, not by the extent of their direct use by the few, but by the consequences of this limited use to the many. So long as all the facts can be had, we can check up on the experts whenever we want to take the time and trouble. Meanwhile, we can let them do the hard work for us and give us the benefit of their findings. That is, after all, what experts are for.

As the reader looks over our brief list of sources of information, he will doubtless think of other items that might well be included. The list is, of course, far from exhaustive, and the particular things mentioned are merely a few of the best. The fact that stands out, however, is that no unusual amount of reading need be done to keep ourselves amply informed on the day to day developments of the defense program. It is in connection with the larger aspects of mobilization that the more serious difficulties arise.

When we decided to build a defense economy, just what did we undertake to do? Is there such a thing as mobilization without inflation? If so, should we try to achieve it? Or is inflation necessary, and perhaps even desirable? Possibly, violent inflation is bad, but moderate inflation good. Is there any way to be sure? Should we try to conduct mobilization on a "pay-as-you-go" basis, or should part of the cost be deferred until some future time? Can either one be done? If so, how? Is there any limit to the taxes that people should be asked to pay? Can high taxes hurt anyone except the people taxed? Are some taxes preferable to others during defense mobilization? Is there any need for price controls? If so, under what conditions? Is there any sense in rationing consumer goods? Is it justifiable often, or seldom, or never?

These questions and many others like them are bound to arise in the minds of more and more people as defense mobilization continues. If our program is to succeed, such questions must be answered, and not by official edict, either. The people of this country are strongly unimpressed by voices of authority. Americans have always done their own thinking in good times and bad, and the results are by no means discouraging. The economics of defense is a complicated subject, and most of us are willing to leave much of it to the experts. On the other hand, we do not care to have our experts tampering with the national economy unless they can give us a satisfactory accounting of their performance at brief intervals. Few people want to be professional economists, but everyone would like to feel sure that he knows enough about the subject to justify confidence in his own judgments.

So far as defense mobilization is concerned, this much economic competence may be readily had. In recent years, economists have been developing a new technique of analysis that is in many ways an improvement on earlier methods. Although the new technique has limitations that will be obvious enough to everyone, it does make it possible to show in a rough way how the whole economic system operates under a variety of conditions, which is exactly what most of us want to know.

The Model Technique

When an inventor believes that he has succeeded in developing a new thing or a new way of doing an old thing, he tests his idea by means of a working model. The model provides a crucial test of the invention. If it works, the invention is at least sound in itself, though it may be neither new nor profitable. In the physical sciences, use has long been made of a similar technique. Astronomers, for instance, have constructed simple models of the solar system in which the planets move around the sun, the whole set-up being composed of sticks and bits of string. Chemists and physicists, too, have made up models of atoms and molecules, displaying very clearly their ideas concerning the nature of these things.

Economists have recently been working out a number of models that have much in common with those used in the older sciences. Some highly ingenious pieces of equipment have been devised, showing in three dimensions how the American economy functions, and how various changes in one part of it will affect all the other parts. Naturally, no such mechanical contraptions can give more than a rudimentary idea of the economic activities of many millions of people, but it is remarkable how many important economic principles they can display.

In this book, we shall not attempt to construct even as elaborate models as could be shown in two dimensions. The sensible rule to observe in building economic models is to make them only as complicated as the analysis requires. The diagrams that can be drawn are not strikingly realistic at best, and any attempt to include unessential details merely creates needless difficulties. A very simple diagram can show the basic features of an economic system, and with the aid of such diagrams a great deal of light can be shed on the major problems of defense mobilization.

Since all the analysis undertaken in this book makes use of the model technique, a word about its application is in order. The best and easiest way to follow the discussion is to make a rough sketch of the model referred to, and check the points made against this sketch as the analysis proceeds. The diagrams are so simple that the reader can soon dispense with his sketches, and readily visualize all the relationships being considered. Any difficulties that arise can then be quickly cleared up by sketching the diagram again.

A great advantage of the model technique is that it enables everyone to observe for himself all the effects that are said to take place. Nothing has to be taken on faith; the reader can test every statement for himself, and see just what he thinks of it. Since the discussion in this book is concerned with basic principles rather than with details, the reader will also be able to supply additional points and qualifications as he proceeds. Better still, the model technique makes it easy to work out correct answers to questions that have not yet arisen in connection with mobilization, as well as to other questions of general economic interest.

Chapter 2

THE PEACETIME ECONOMY

The American Economy was once designated simply as "capitalism." As the role of government has grown in importance, however, some rather more colorful terms have become popular. Such expressions as "state capitalism," "the laboristic economy," "the welfare state," and "the farewell state" seem to have little in common, but all of them and a variety of others have been applied to the United States. Since history is a one-way street, American capitalism can never again be quite what it used to be, but it is safe to say that our economy is still capitalist, at least in comparison with that of most other countries in the world.

The object of this chapter is to develop a model of the American economy in peacetime, and for this purpose the question of terminology is not of vital importance. We may call the system whatever we choose; our problem is to show how it works. To reveal in detail precisely how American capitalism functions would be too ambitious a task, for this is something that economists are still trying to find out. Fortunately, a more modest effort will suffice. All we need is a simple model that will emphasize especially those broad features of the peacetime economy that distinguish it most from a war or defense economy.

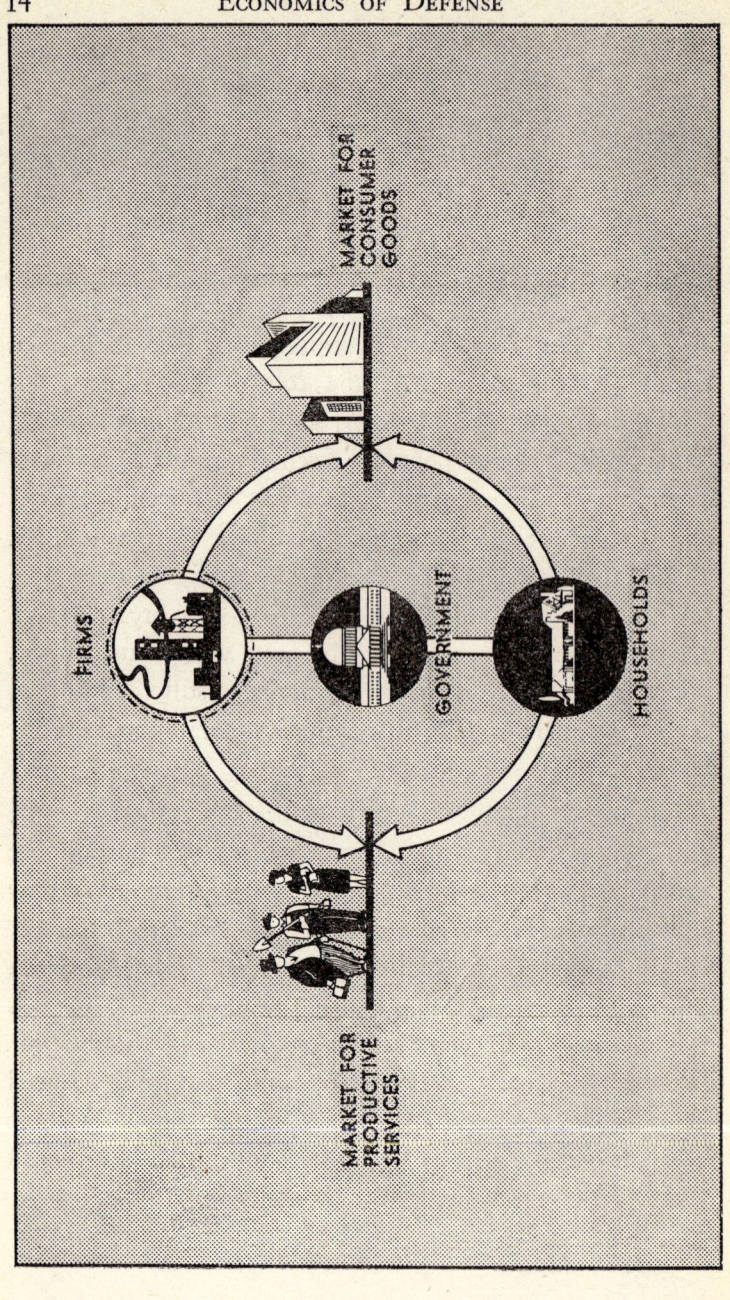

Figure 2.1. THE PEACETIME ECONOMY.

The Model

Figure 2.1 is our model of the American Economy in peacetime. Like a road map or blueprint, the diagram means little in itself. To make use of any of these things, we must first discover how to read it and what it is supposed to show. The rest of this chapter will therefore be devoted to a discussion of the model and the relationships it represents.

If the reader will now make a rough sketch of the diagram, he can refer to that result, rather than to Figure 2.1 as the discussion proceeds. This will not merely save the trouble of turning pages back and forth; a sketch, with a few labels and notes to accompany it, can serve as an excellent summary of the entire chapter. After going through the first few chapters in this way, the reader will find that he can follow the rest of the discussion with very few references to diagrams, and that he has acquired an effective technique for handling many different economic questions.

Production

In the American capitalist economy, production is carried on by both private enterprises and government agencies. Business firms (proprietorships, partnerships, and corporations) produce goods and services for private profit. Local, state, and national governments employ large numbers of persons who produce comparatively few tangible goods, but who perform a great variety of services for the public as a whole.

Our model shows all firms grouped into a single area at the top of a large circle. The area itself lies between two markets: A Market for Productive Services on one side, and a Market for Consumer Goods on the other. Firms deal with households through both these markets. Through the Market for Productive Services, firms buy from households the labor services and other resources required for production. Through the Market for Consumer Goods, firms sell to households goods and services emerging from the productive process. As we look at our model, we can imagine that a great stream of labor and resources is flowing into the area containing firms; that this stream is broken up into many smaller ones as the various stages of production are carried on; and that consumer goods keep flowing out of the area to be bought by households.

Although private production includes all kinds of profit-seeking activity, we may split the total into two major categories:

1. *The production of goods and services for immediate sale to consumers, and of the raw materials and semi-finished products that go directly into these consumer goods.*

2. *All other production.* This consists of buildings, machinery, and equipment that are not intended for consumer use, but that are used by the firms themselves in the productive process. Also included are any products added to stocks of goods in the hands of firms, whether destined for future sale to consumers or not.

Looking at our model, we can see why the distinction between these two types of production is worth making. As firms buy productive services from households, and use these services to turn out a stream of products, not all the output being produced at any given time is necessarily reaching the Market for Consumer Goods. Besides the consumer goods that do pass to households through this market, there may be a large or small volume of other products that stay within the area containing the firms. From the standpoint of all the firms combined, the accumulation of goods within this area represents *investment*. Money is being invested in additional stocks of raw materials, finished products, and goods in partly finished form when inventories increase. Money is also being invested when firms expand their productive facilities by increasing their plant and equipment. As investment in inventories and increased productive capacity takes place, we can imagine that the area containing our firms grows larger. A dotted line around the area suggests this effect, and we shall shortly be ready to develop its significance.

Consumption

The goods and services sold by firms through the Market for Consumer Goods are bought and used by individuals, families, and other groups. These households are not entirely different people from those composing the firms. Our model shows them in a separate area because they are doing something different, but the population of the United States as a whole naturally does both the producing and the consuming. Since consuming is the opposite of producing, we have placed the households opposite the firms in our model, and this brings them into an opposite relationship to the markets in the system.

In the Market for Productive Services, firms are the buyers, and households are the sellers. By the sale to firms of labor services, property rights in land, and other productive wealth, households become the employes, creditors, and owners of particular firms, and thus earn their money incomes.

In the Market for Consumer Goods, households are the buyers, and firms the sellers. As any given household spends money through this market, the money goes first to some firm, but much of it soon becomes income to the households whose members compose that firm. Apart from the activities of government, the operation of the peacetime economy may thus be described in terms of a circular flow of money in one direction, and of goods and services in the other. Before considering the place of government in the system, let us examine this basic circular flow a little more carefully.

The Income Stream

As we look at our model, we can imagine that our firms and households are connected by a circular income stream. Money income flows from firms to households through the Market for Productive Services, and returns to firms through the Market for Consumer Goods. At the same time, a flow of real income in the form of goods and services ready for use moves around the circle in the opposite direction. The labor and resources of households are sold to firms, converted into producer goods to be used in further production and consumer goods for more immediate use by households, and a stream of output available for consumption flows into the household area. Notice that the material wellbeing of households depends not only on the money they earn in the Market for Productive Services, but also on what is available in the Market for Consumer Goods.

In the Market for Consumer Goods a stream of output meets the stream of household expenditure. The relative magnitude of these two streams determines the price level of consumer goods. If more money is spent by households on a given flow of output, this price level rises; if less is spent relative to output, this price level falls.

In the Market for Productive Services another general price level is similarly determined. Both the major markets, however, are composed of thousands of smaller ones in each of which a stream of expenditure meets a stream of specific goods or services. Although the two general price levels are of some interest, we are usually more concerned about changes in the smaller regions. In a discussion of wage changes and their effects, for instance, the labor market rather than the whole Market for Productive Services is relevant.

Saving and Investment

We are now ready to observe some of the fundamental features of the American economy in peacetime, and to see in a general way how the whole system operates. In order to clarify the picture, we shall ignore the role of government for the time being, and focus our attention on the firms and households that compose the private sphere. The role of government can, in any event, be properly developed only by showing how government activities affect the rest of the economy, and logical analysis thus requires a treatment of the private sector first.

Looking at our model, let us begin by raising a basic question. Do the households in a capitalist system earn enough money to buy all the output they produce? Since all the households combined are the employes, creditors, and owners of all the firms combined, it appears that the answer must be *yes*. As goods are produced, their costs of production are the wages, salaries, interest, and so on that firms pay to households through the Market for Productive Services, and the profits that firms make on their operations belong to the owners of the firms. It might seem, therefore, that the circular flow of real and money income ought to be a smooth and steady stream, with households always buying everything produced, and with firms always just selling their whole output. As everyone knows, however, this is far from being what happens. Taking firms as a whole, we know that business is always getting either better or worse, and that there is hardly any such thing as steady business conditions. From the standpoint of households, conditions are always changing too. Their total incomes are either increasing or decreasing, and so are their expenditures. Why should this be so?

We have now arrived at the problem of economic fluctuations. Nobody has yet found the whole answer to this problem, but economists are agreed that a good deal of light can be shed on it by a study of the relation of saving to investment. Through the whole course of American history, the economy has either been expanding, with rising levels of income, output, employment, and prices, or contracting, with the falling levels characteristic of recession or depression. When we treat the operation of the peacetime economy in terms of saving and investment, it is thus prosperity and depression that we have to explain.

As we look back over the economic history of the United States, we are struck immediately by the tremendous change and growth that have occurred. If we are led to suspect that there is some fundamental connection between this process of development and the capitalist nature of our economy, we shall be quite right. Capitalism is not a static condition; it is a dynamic process of change and expansion. Profit-seeking firms continually introduce new products and new techniques of production, creating new industries, and revolutionizing old ones. The waves of investment to which this process gives rise generate new income that expands the whole circular flow, thus yielding periods of prosperity. When investment slackens prosperity gives way to recession, and income, output, employment, and prices tend to decline until another wave of development occurs.

In our model, we can see how all this takes place. Starting with the households, we have a stream of money flowing through the Market for Consumer Goods, and into the area containing the firms. As this money reaches the firms, not much of it leaves the area immediately to become household income again. Most of it instead passes from one firm to another in payment for raw materials, supplies, and equipment needed to renew what is depreciating. At any given time, however, the total flow of income out of the area is equal to the flow into it if current production is just equal to current consumption. In other words, the money coming in from households equals that going out again to households, if there are no changes in the stocks of goods and the plant and equipment held by the firms.

As long as total production just equals total consumption, all the firms put together are creating the same amount of income for households in the Market for Productive Services that households are paying to firms through the Market for Consumer Goods. In periods of rapid development, firms are building up their plant and equipment, and are creating new productive capacity for future use. Production therefore exceeds current consumption, and household earnings are greater than their expenditures on consumer goods. As firms invest for future returns, they inject new income into the circular flow. This money invested by firms may be obtained by them from their own past saving, or more likely from the sale of securities to households or by borrowing from banks. In any event, increases in investment increase household income, and further effects then follow.

As household earnings increase, it is likely that households will wish to save part of their additional income. Some households may want to save all of it, but taking them all together, we may safely say that total spending on consumer goods is going to increase. As increases in household spending begin to reach the firms through the Market for Consumer Goods, the firms will be encouraged to invest still more money in building up stocks of goods and in expansions of existing plant and equipment. As production expands, income and employment increase, and prices rise too as households increase their spending faster than the additional consumer goods come onto the market. Every increase in investment increases household income, and every increase in household spending tends to encourage further investment. A comparatively small wave of original investment may thus set in motion a cumulative process of expansion that will produce capitalist prosperity for a number of years.

To see why prosperity always gives way to recession sooner or later we may turn to the question of saving. All the households put together are said to save to the extent that they spend less than their total income on consumption. Saving is, of course, often defined in other ways; this particular definition is used because it makes the analysis easy to handle. In the model, then, households "save" any income that they earn in the Market for Productive Services but do not spend in the Market for Consumer Goods. The money thus "saved" may be used to buy securities from firms, and may turn up shortly as investment. Or, it may be put into banks, held by households themselves, or otherwise disposed of. We shall not allow it to go to government for taxes, simply because government is not being included in this analysis, and we want to see how things work quite independently of government action. The significant point about saving is that, whatever may happen to the money later on, it has been withdrawn from the immediately existing income stream.

Looking at our model, we can visualize the nature of the saving-investment relationship very easily. Investment injects money into the income stream at the top; saving draws money out at the bottom. When investment is greater than saving, the new money that firms put into the income stream is not all withdrawn. The part not saved goes on around the circle, increasing the income of firms from the sale of consumer goods. A continuous excess of investment over saving is therefore a way of describing the increases in income characteristic of periods of prosperity. A persistent excess of saving over investment implies the opposite.

Now, as household income keeps rising in prosperity, household spending on consumer goods keeps increasing, but saving increases too. Investment injects more income into the circular flow; spending on consumer goods maintains the income flow; saving draws income out of the system. If any given amount of investment is injected into the income stream at each round of the wheel, cumulative expansion follows only if less than this is saved. Since households save more on each round as their incomes increase, a point is bound to be reached at which they draw as much income out of the circular flow as the firms are injecting. Beyond this level income cannot rise any further. In fact, at this point, income not merely stops rising, but starts to fall. When consumer spending stops increasing, firms cut down their investment in new plant and equipment, and a period of recession, or even considerable depression, follows.

During recessions, saving continually runs ahead of investment, with income accordingly falling, output shrinking, and unemployment growing. We shall not pause to develop the details of this process, for, as we shall see, peacetime prosperity sheds much more light on the problem of defense mobilization than does recession or depression. It may be worthwhile, however, to comment on one question that nearly always arises in connection with saving and investment. Does prosperity give way to recession because investment is too small or because saving is too large?

Sometimes this question is answered one way, and sometimes the other. There is much less difference of opinion among economists, however, than this would suggest. Most students of the problem agree that what happens in prosperity is a gradual increase in investment, followed by a much more rapid increase as the cumulative expansion develops, and then comparatively small increases as prosperity approaches an end. It is only when investment begins to slacken that saving catches up to it, and if there were either more investment or less saving prosperity would continue. Of the two, however, the more dynamic factor is investment. As the progress of science and invention creates new physical possibilities, many of these open profit opportunities to business firms that are willing to take a chance on them. The money that such firms invest is sufficient, if neither a boom nor a recession is already in full swing, to raise the level of the income stream appreciably, and start a cumulative process of expansion and prosperity. As new projects are completed, and new products and processes become part of the changing scene, the pace of investment tends to slacken, and prosperity gives way to recession and depression. After a more or less painful interlude of general readjustment, the stage is set for another wave of capitalist development, and prosperity gradually emerges again.

The Price System

An outstanding feature of the peacetime American economy, and one that is in marked contrast to socialist, communist, and fascist states, is the absence of centralized control and direction of the everyday business affairs of the people. This feature of the American economy is sufficiently familiar to everyone, but not everyone fully appreciates its implications. From the standpoint of the economist, it is precisely this familiar fact that makes the study of Amercan capitalism so interesting and so difficult. When we are studying a socialist state, for instance, we want to know what plans the central authority is making, and how these plans are working out, but we never have to wonder how the whole economy manages to hang together, or why it should be capable of working at all.

A planned economy is comparable to a branch of the armed forces. There may be a few privates in the Army who question their own ability to be Chief of Staff, but there can be hardly any privates who are ignorant of how, in principle, the whole show operates. The Company Commander is immediately to blame, but he gets his orders from higher up, and so do his superiors as far as they go. What makes the whole thing function can be no mystery when every man is told what to do, and someone is responsible for making him do it.

In calling the American peacetime economy planless, we naturally do not mean to deny that both private groups and governmental agencies make numerous plans and try to carry these plans into effect. The essential point is that plans of this sort are made with a large number of different ends in view, and that there is no master plan for the whole economy into which all the smaller programs must fit. Without centralized planning and coordination, the peacetime economy must run itself automatically through the price system.

The price system is much more than a mere set of prices; it is part of a complex structure of interdependent prices, incomes, expenditures, and rates of output. When we refer to the price system, then, we really have in mind the whole scheme of interlocking relationships that both affect prices and are affected by them. If the price system is to accomplish what would otherwise require centralized planning and control, it must do at least three things. *First,* it must guide production, leading individual firms to produce the things that people will buy, and in the appropriate amounts. *Second,* it must get the labor and resources of the country into the hands of particular firms, directing more toward those whose products are in greater demand, and less toward others. *Third,* as all the different goods and services emerge from the productive process, each must be rationed to its users, the quantity each user gets being somehow determined. Let us see, with the aid of our model, how the price system manages to do these things.

We may begin by supposing that the research department of one of our firms develops some new product, and that the management must decide whether or not to manufacture and sell it to consumers. The decision depends mainly on the prospect that the product will yield profits to the firm, and this in turn is a question of prices. The firm must buy labor and resources in the Market for Productive Services, and the prices of these things will govern the cost of production. The firm must sell the product in the Market for Consumer Goods, and must be able to compete with other firms for a share of total household expenditure. At a high price, sales will be small; at a low price, they will be larger. The price, however, cannot be below production costs, though the costs may depend to some extent on the volume of sales. Clearly, the management has to solve a difficult problem, and the outcome cannot be known with perfect certainty. The point to notice, however, is that the calculations of the management rest on the relations between prices in the two markets, the price system serving as a guide to what will be produced.

Let us now assume that the new product is manufactured and put on the market. If consumers find it preferable to older products, they will shift their spending from the old goods to the new. Firms producing the older products may cut their prices in order to maintain sales, but prices can be cut only so far without getting below production costs and turning profits into losses. The price system may thus prevent old firms from continuing to produce less favored goods and may force them to concentrate their efforts on something else or go out of business altogether. In either event, the labor and resources of the economy get shifted out of their former uses and into new ones.

Finally, let us observe that the price at which the new product is sold serves to equalize production and consumption, and to ration the output among consumers. If consumers buy the product faster than it can be produced, the firm either raises its price or expands production until orderly operations are achieved. Whatever the rate of output finally arrived at, the product goes only to consumers who are able and willing to pay the price being charged, and those who do not want it or cannot afford it go without.

Government

With our brief glimpse of the price system, we have completed our survey of the private part of the peacetime economy, and are ready to consider the role of government. We are using the term *Government* to cover all the local, state, and national agencies that affect the functioning of the economy, but the Federal government is the most important of these, and it is the one we shall have mainly in mind.

In the United States, Government owns and operates

comparatively few enterprises directly. The Post Office, the Tennessee Valley Authority, the Reconstruction Finance Corporation, and similar businesses are exceptions to the general rule, and even such businesses are not operated in a completely businesslike way. The affairs of Government are conducted, not primarily with a view to making profits, but rather for the general wellbeing of the American people. For the most part, we may think of the relation of Government to the private economy as having two major aspects:

1. Government makes and enforces the laws and rules under which private firms and households must act. Although Government regulation of the economy has been increasing for a long time, it has never amounted to highly centralized planning and control more than temporarily. The contrast between peace and war is what stands out, and this is sufficiently familiar to require no special comment.

2. For us, at present, the more important aspect of Government is the one shown by our model. In carrying on its activities, Government spends large sums of money, and this money goes into the income stream to become private income. At the same time, Government levies taxes on both firms and households, and draws large amounts of money out of the income stream. Let us look into this a little further with the aid of our model.

Starting with Government expenditure, we can imagine two streams of money flowing out of the Government area; one going to firms, and the other to households. The flow to firms represents payments for the goods bought by Government from private enterprises; the flow to households consists mainly of the wages and salaries of employes on the public payroll.

Government receipts in the form of taxes flow into the Government area from both firms and households. As firms produce goods and services, Government levies taxes on the manufacture and sale of numerous products. Government likewise taxes the profits made by firms. From households Government collects personal income taxes in particular, as well as various other fees.

As we can easily see in our model, the effect of Government taxing and spending is to shift income around within the economy from one firm and household to another. We can also see less easily that Government taxing and spending may raise or lower the level of the whole income stream. If the flow of taxes into the Government area is larger than the flow of expenditure out of the area, part of the income drawn from the circular flow fails to get back again immediately, and the stream of income shrinks. This is the condition known to historians as a Government surplus.

More familiar to most of us is the condition of Government deficit. When the taxes collected by Government are not sufficient to cover all expenditures, the flow out of the Government area exceeds the flow into it, and the level of the income stream is raised. To get the extra money, Government borrows by selling bonds to firms, households, and banks. We have omitted banks from our model of the peacetime economy, not because they are unimportant, but because their importance can be developed more effectively at a later point. For the time being, it is sufficient to think of banks as lying anywhere outside the circular flow, since all that matters is that the money borrowed from them was not already in the income stream.

Chapter 3

THE WAR ECONOMY

A War Economy and a peacetime economy are not two completely different systems. They are rather the same basic system functioning under different conditions. In the present chapter we shall take the similarities largely for granted in order to concentrate our attention on the contrasts and lay a better basis for the analysis of defense mobilization. When we come to examine the defense economy we shall deal with most of the problems that arise when the system is functioning in all-out war. Details may therefore be omitted for the time being.

The Model

Figure 3.1 is our model of the war economy. As we should expect, it resembles our model of the peacetime economy in its basic structure. Firms, households, and government again appear; the same two markets are present; and the circular flow of economic activity goes on much as before. Let us now observe the contrasts.

To begin with, the role of government is greatly expanded in wartime, and this is suggested by the increased size of the government area. Next, the area containing firms has been split into two parts. Production for war is distinguished from civilian production, though the separation is not perfectly clear cut. Food and clothing, for instance, may be produced for either the armed forces or

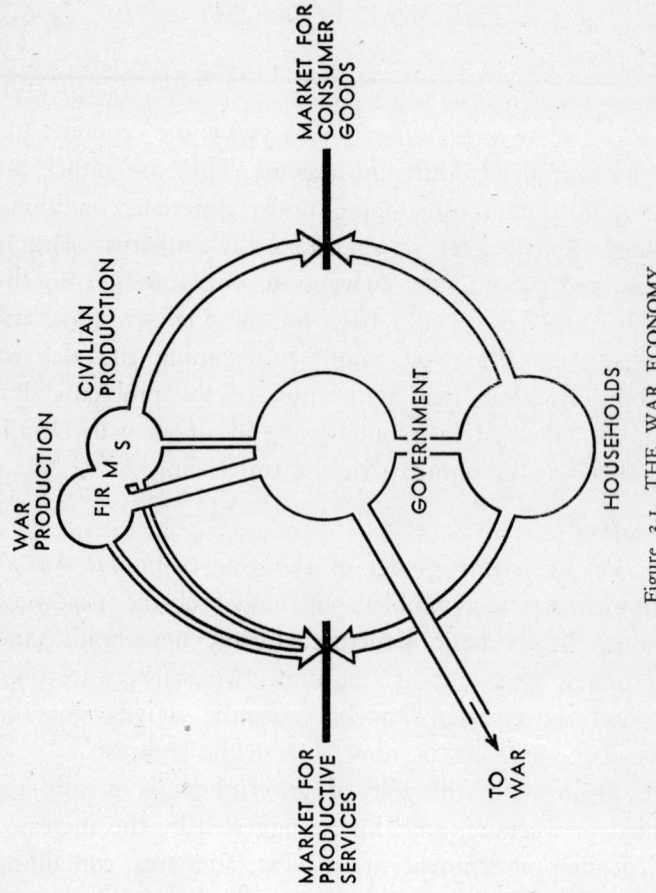

Figure 3.1. THE WAR ECONOMY.

civilians or both. The thing to notice is that Government becomes the buyer of the war output, and that the productive capacity left for civilian goods is substantially reduced. If much productive capacity had been idle before the war, as was true at the beginning of World War II, the total *output* of civilian goods would not necessarily be reduced very much. The production of certain specific civilian goods would be cut back, as resources were shifted into war production, but the utilization of idle plant and equipment could give more households employment, and maintain the total flow of civilian goods at nearly the former level.

Our model of the war economy brings out a final fact: The war goods bought by Government go out of the system altogether, but the money spent by Government goes into the income stream. This fact is not wholly in contrast to Government purchasing in peacetime; the goods that Government ordinarily buys seldom reappear in private markets anyway. The really significant difference is in the size of the effect. In World War II, Government was buying at times as much as all the households put together, and when purchases are on such a scale the destination of the goods is a matter of the first importance.

The American Economy in Wartime

Before we analyze the operation of the war economy with the aid of our model, let us notice the conditions in which it has to function.

1. The goal of a war economy is obviously to win a war. In American experience there has always been the further aim of maintaining as many as possible of our traditional

liberties during the war. In the economic sphere, this means that efforts have always been made to preserve such essential features of the peacetime system as would not jeopardize our chances of victory.

This sort of split objective accounts for many of the peculiar features of the American economy in time of war. The reason for the divided character of the objective is, however, easy to understand. The American people have fought wars in modern times in order to ward off what they have regarded as dangerous threats to their way of life, and they naturally do not propose to begin a war by deliberately destroying this way of life themselves. On the other hand, as war goes on everyone is aware that victory is the first necessity, and that mere survival may require the temporary sacrifice of other ends. With the shifting fortunes of war, we thus emphasize first one part of our double goal and then the other.

2. Since winning an all-out war requires the collective efforts of the entire population, centralized planning is an essential feature of the war economy. In the United States, the planning is done by government agencies of great number and variety. These agencies are co-ordinated through the executive branch of the government under the President, who not only serves as Commander in Chief of the armed forces, but exercises special war powers granted by Congress.

Although the war powers of the President make him virtually a dictator over the American economy, the exercise of these powers has always been limited to what most people have accepted as necessary to the successful conduct of war. The co-ordination of planning, too, has never been carried to the point where all civilian and military requirements were simultaneously determined and provided for. The failure to perfect centralized planning in wartime has obvious drawbacks, but it also possesses the advantage of insuring that not all the government agencies will be making the same mistake at the same time.

3. In the war economy, the plans made by Government are carried out partly through the price system and partly by direct action in which the price system is short-circuited. We shall have occasion to examine these means of controlling economic activities in connection with defense mobilization, but we may make one observation at this point. In general, plans that involve comparatively small and slow changes can be carried out well through the price system; plans that involve large and rapid changes cannot. Since examples will be discussed later on, we need only suggest the reason for this now. As our earlier discussion of the price system may have shown, price changes serve as an inducement to firms and households to act in some way; but changes in prices do not compel any particular people to do anything at any definite time.

Production and Consumption

In the war economy, Government tries to achieve a balance of resources among three things: The size of the armed forces, war production, and civilian production. The number of men in each of the armed services, for example, is dependent not so much on the number fitted to serve as on the number that can be steadily furnished with weapons and supplies out of the productive capacity of the nation. Since every member of the Army, Navy, or Air

Force is one person taken from the production of war or civilian goods, it is clear that the problem is anything but simple. To make matters more complicated, the civilian population must be maintained at a level of living that will not impair its efficiency to produce the goods needed for war. The "necessities" allowed civilians are therefore not the things they cannot and should not do without, but those they will not do without while producing efficiently. Labor and resources that "go to waste" in keeping civilians supplied with "non-essentials" in wartime may reflect intelligent decisions on the part of Government planners.

In the war economy, total production tends to be at a maximum. As our model shows, only a part of the total consists of civilian goods; the rest is war production bought by Government. This means that civilians are producing many more goods than are available for them to consume. An excess of production over consumption occurs in peacetime through the process of investment that we discussed in the preceding chapter. The effect of Government purchases in wartime is similar to this, but on a vastly greater scale.

In the war economy, civilians earn enough income to buy not only the civilian goods they produce but all the war output as well. There is thus an enormous gap between the total amount of money that consumers have to spend and the total amount that civilian output would ordinarily be worth. In other words, households have much more money to spend on consumption than would buy the whole output of consumer goods at current prices. This excess of purchasing power creates a so-called "inflationary gap" in the Market for Consumer Goods, since the spending of more money on a given flow of output raises the price level in this market. The problem of inflation is one of the most serious that arise in either a war or defense economy, and we shall devote the whole of Chapter 6 to it. Meanwhile, we may observe that Government tries in wartime to get excess income away from households by taxing them heavily and by selling bonds to them.

War Finance

Government taxes households and sells bonds to them mainly to keep them from spending too much money on the limited output of consumer goods. At the same time, the money that Government thus gets from households helps to pay for the war goods that Government buys from firms. Government also raises money by levying new taxes on the profits of firms, and the production and sale of civilian goods. If Government collected in taxes as much as it was spending, the war would be conducted on a "pay-as-you-go" basis, and Government would emerge from the war with no increase in the bond issues that compose the public debt.

Wars have never in fact been wholly financed by the pay-as-you-go method. Government has always spent more on wars than it has collected in taxes during the wars, and the national debt has always increased in wartime as Government borrowed both from the general public and from banks. We shall consider why this should have been so in connection with the problems of mobilization, but we should note that the extent to which a war is paid for as it occurs is entirely a financial question. All wars must be wholly paid for as they occur in terms of the real efforts and sacrifices of the people concerned. The members of a war economy do all the work and put all the resources into the goods consumed by the war, and there is no way in which the nation as a whole can shift any of this cost onto future generations. Different methods of financing a war may be thought of as different ways of sharing the immediate burden among the people of the country.

In addition to the immediate cost of wars, there are, of course, after-effects that may last for many years. Indeed, it can hardly be said that any nation, after fighting a major war, is ever in quite the same condition as if the war had not occurred. Lives and resources consumed by wars are never really "made up for" afterward, and war finance has consequences that extend into the remote future.

Chapter 4

THE DEFENSE ECONOMY

As we have already seen, the defense economy cannot be thought of as the final end product of mobilization. We may distinguish, if we please, between the process of building and the thing we are trying to build, but we can never regard the process as finished and the structure as complete. A peacetime economy lies behind us in the past; a war economy may be forced upon us in the future. We cannot safely go back to the first, and we have no desire to go on to the second. We must therefore keep on building our defense economy, and we must make it operate while we are building it.

The object of the present chapter is to develop a model of the defense economy, and to notice the problems that arise in building and operating it. In the chapters that follow, we shall discuss these problems one by one, analyzing the various methods of dealing with them.

The Model

Figure 4.1 is our model of the defense economy. The model is reproduced in skeleton form in Figure 4.2, together with similar skeletons of the peacetime and wartime models. As we should expect, the three models look much alike. All of them represent the American economic system, and the differences merely emphasize the distinctions with which our analysis is chiefly concerned. We may remark

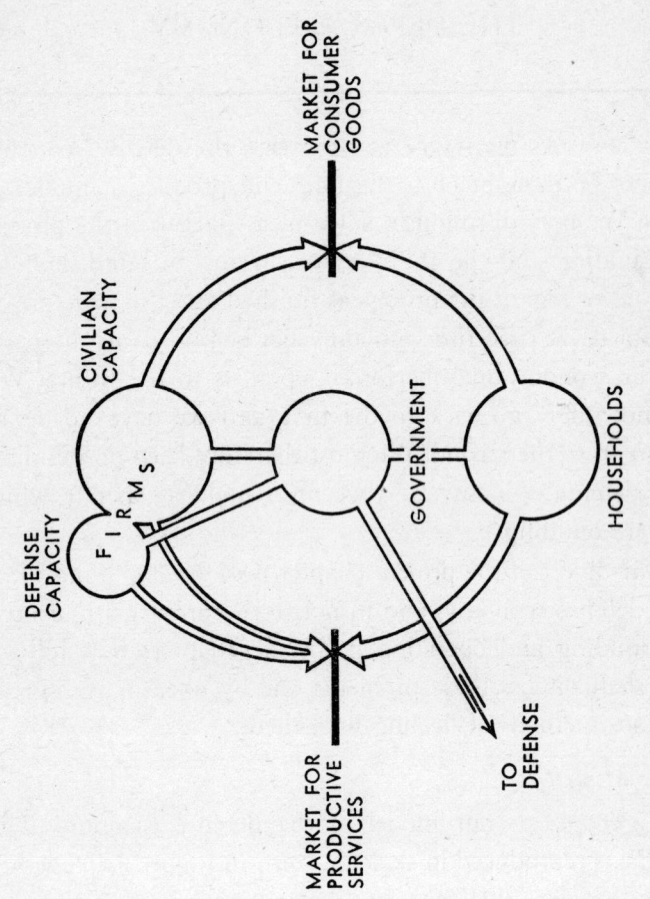

Figure 4.1. THE DEFENSE ECONOMY.

in passing that these differences are largely matters of degree. The features that stand out in a war or defense economy are not totally absent in peacetime, and the elaboration of parallels would be instructive. To people who must conduct their affairs in one economy or another, however, the contrasts are more striking and significant. Let us begin by observing those brought out by the models themselves.

The area labelled "Defense Capacity" in our model of the defense economy resembles that called "War Production" in the wartime model. The difference, while it is hardly visible on the diagrams, is nonetheless important. In the war economy, war production tends to take place at the expense of civilian production, and a large share of existing productive capacity is shifted from peacetime to war production. In the defense economy, on the contrary, we are trying to build up the area representing defense capacity without cutting down the size of the area representing civilian output. Although we realize that the production of some specific civilian goods must be cut as labor and resources are shifted to the defense area, we hope to maintain the flow of civilian output as a whole, reductions in some items being offset by increases in others.

The size of the Government area is larger in the defense economy than in peacetime, but smaller than in the war economy. This difference in the models corresponds to the different magnitude of the role of Government in the three sets of circumstances. Government is related to the two groups of firms in the defense economy much as in the war economy, but the purchase and immediate consumption of goods by Government is smaller in the defense model.

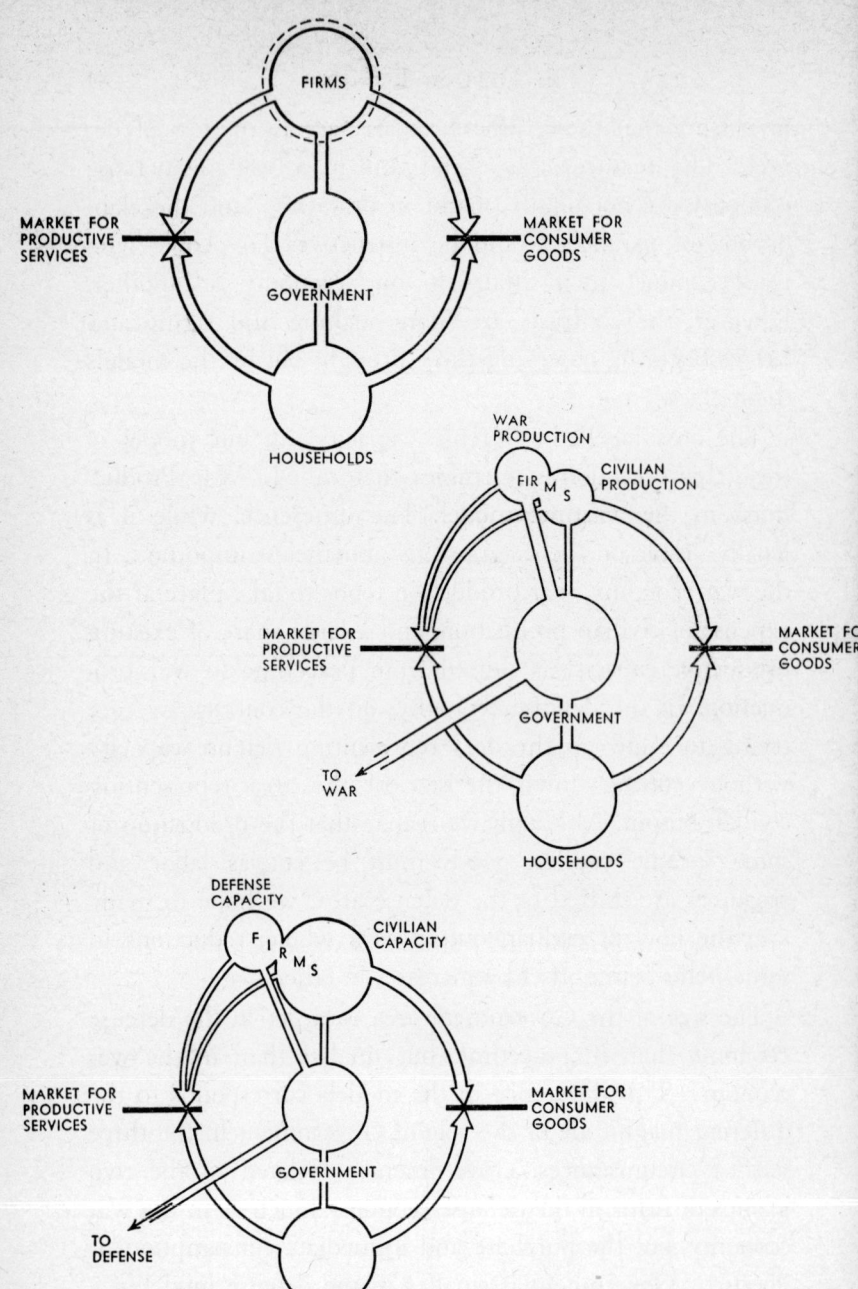

Figure 4.2. THE THREE MODELS.

The Economy During Mobilization

Let us follow the order of treatment that we adopted for the war economy, and notice next the conditions in which the defense model must function.

1. The goal of the defense economy is to prepare the nation for all-out war while leaving all possible features of the peacetime economy intact. As in a war economy, we thus have a split objective, but there are important differences. A war economy is essentially temporary; it functions under conditions of extreme emergency that cannot be expected to last. Resources are poured into the conflict at a rate far greater than could be permanently maintained, and sacrifices are made that could not be repeated. People can give their lives and property but once, and can work at top speed for only limited periods of time. A war economy is geared to a pace at which the nation would soon approach exhaustion; the defense economy must function for the indefinite future. In the defense economy, then, resources are accumulated rather than spent, and people are called upon to make few sacrifices of the extreme character appropriate in wartime.

2. Since a collective goal exists for defense mobilization, the defense economy is subject to centralized planning. Government agencies are charged with the responsibility for building the new structure, and must deal with the problems of mobilization as they arise. A good deal of planning is done only on paper, for Government has to be ready to change its program, shifting from a defense to a war economy if this should become necessary. The role of Government is larger in the defense economy than in the peacetime economy, not merely because Government is al-

ready doing more, but because it is also getting ready to do more.

3. In the defense economy, the plans of Government agencies are carried out partly through the price system, and partly by direct action. The price system is used to a larger extent than it is in a war economy, but it is short-circuited by direct controls as well.

With these considerations in mind, we may now return to our model for a preliminary survey of the economics of defense.

Production

Government tries, even in peacetime, to keep workers employed and productive capacity in use. In the defense economy, as in time of war, maximum production is of prime importance, for losses of output that we could afford in peacetime can no longer be tolerated. In contrast to wartime, however, the production of actual arms and war equipment is not very large during defense mobilization. As this is written, we are conducting operations in Korea that amount to war on a considerable scale. To those directly involved, things are as bad as they would be if the whole nation were struggling for survival; indeed, in some ways worse, for their sacrifices are not being so generally matched by others. If little attention is paid to the Korean conflict in this book, it is not because it is undeserving of notice. It is simply because, for the purpose of our analysis, we are viewing it as part of a larger effort that is treated as a whole. In our model, the flow of output shown going "to defense" includes that being consumed in the Korean action as well as that going into the arming of ourselves and our allies. We are treating this total flow, rather than any of its component parts, and even the total is small in comparison with the similar flow in a war economy.

In a war economy, emphasis is placed on the immediate output of war goods, and war production may be increased largely at the expense of civilian output. In the defense economy, emphasis is placed not on immediate war production but on the production of more and better equipment with which to produce war goods in the future. We are hoping, moreover, to create the new productive capacity without cutting the output of civilian goods as a whole. How may this be done?

As we saw in our discussion of the peacetime economy, the area containing firms in that model grows larger as new firms are organized, and as old firms install additional plant and equipment. The total volume of new investment of this sort varies from time to time, and is closely associated with the alternating periods of general economic expansion and contraction that make up business cycles. Now, if production as a whole can be kept close to the sort of maximum levels approached in peacetime prosperities, a substantial part of total output can be used to increase defense capacity instead of increasing the capacity of firms to produce civilian goods. To build defense capacity then, we need give up little that we already have. Our aggregate sacrifice can be measured only vaguely in terms of the further things that we might otherwise have had.

Building defense capacity is comparable to the peacetime process of investment, and it has many of the same effects. As the defense economy begins to take shape, we experience a "mobilization boom" that accounts for many of the problems with which Government has to deal.

Consumption

Although total consumption need not be materially reduced in the defense economy, the output of some consumer goods must be cut to free resources for use in the new defense area. Steel, for example, is used in the manufacture of such consumer goods as automobiles, refrigerators, ranges, and home laundries, but it is also used in the manufacture of the heavy machinery that goes into defense plants. Scarcities of some specific commodities thus develop, even if consumers can buy about as many goods in general as before.

Shortages of a few specific consumer goods create no more serious problems in the defense economy than in peacetime, and the price system provides for the appropriate adjustments. The prices of the scarce items tend to rise, and only those people willing and able to pay the higher prices continue to get the goods. Since we have just pointed out that the production of consumer goods as a whole need not be substantially reduced, it may appear that all is well in this sector of the defense economy. Unfortunately, any such impression would be the reverse of the truth. An overall shortage of consumer goods is exactly the thing that does develop almost as soon as mobilization begins, and this shortage is one of the outstanding features of the whole picture.

Looking at our model, we observe that the money spent in building up defense capacity enters the income stream, increasing household earnings, and leading to increased household spending for consumer goods. So far, the situation resembles that of an ordinary peacetime prosperity very closely. Now, however, we observe an important difference. In the peacetime economy, the prices of consumer goods begin to rise as household spending increases, and the rise in prices is shortly followed by an increase in the production of consumer goods. Since the firms increase output in response to the increased consumer demand, the flow of goods to the market expands more slowly than the consumer spending, and prices continue to rise gradually during the prosperity. In the defense economy, the flow of consumer goods to the market may not be reduced, but neither is it increased. Consequently, as soon as households begin to spend their larger incomes on consumer goods, the prices of the goods begin to rise, and output does not increase to balance the increased spending. Instead, a large "inflationary gap" appears as in a war economy, and the price level of consumer goods may rise enormously.

Problems of Mobilization

In terms of our models, mobilization may be thought of as the process by which we are moving from the peacetime economy to the defense economy. As we have seen, the defense economy is not itself a completed structure, and it functions while the process of mobilization continues. The building and operation of the defense economy may be broken down into a number of different aspects for convenience in discussion, and we may complete this preliminary survey by introducing the topics to be dealt with in subsequent chapters.

1. *Shifting Resources.* In order to build up defense capacity, resources that might otherwise have been used to produce consumer goods or expand civilian goods capacity must be shifted to the new area. How is the shift effected?

What problems are involved? How does Government try to deal with these problems?

2. *Inflation.* We have observed that defense mobilization creates an inflationary gap. Why is this gap a matter of concern? Does it have to be "closed" or not? What does Government do about the inflationary gap? Is the gap actually closed? If so, how? If not, why not?

3. *Indirect Controls.* In directing the building and operation of the defense economy, Government employs as many of the already existing arrangements as possible in order to preserve peacetime conditions to a maximum extent. Since the price system in its broadest sense automatically governs the economic activities of individual firms and households in peacetime, Government agencies try to work through the price system to accomplish their objectives. Taxing, borrowing, buying, and selling may be regarded as indirect controls over the economy. These acts of Government, and others like them, force no particular firms or households to do anything at any particular time. They rather provide strong inducements to people in general to adopt desired courses of action, and thus produce their effects in accustomed ways.

4. *Direct Controls.* Government may issue special regulations and orders when customary methods fail. Since Government in the United States acts mainly in response to the wishes of the governed, direct controls are not invoked casually or merely to save a little trouble for some Government agency. On the contrary, the use of such methods provokes resentment even when most people agree that they are necessary, and resentment is about all that does result unless the need is clear. It is one thing to hand

out a directive, and quite another to enforce it. The conditions under which indirect controls are adequate, and the circumstances in which direct action is called for must be generally agreed upon if the defense economy is to work successfully.

Chapter 5

SHIFTING RESOURCES

DEFENSE MOBILIZATION, as we have seen, requires the building of a sector of new productive capacity for emergency use in place of continuing to enlarge the old sector producing civilian goods. Two things, accordingly, must be done. On the one hand, defense capacity must be built; on the other, civilian capacity must be kept from expanding. Little of the labor and resources flowing into the current production of consumer goods needs to be shifted to the new area, but those that might have been used to increase the size of the old area have to be diverted from it.

In this chapter we shall distinguish between the initial mobilization effort and its consequences. Government must deal with both, but to see what happens, and why, we should start at the beginning and notice how the problems arise.

Use of the Price System

In the early stages of mobilization, Government uses the price system to the maximum extent, and begins to resort to other methods of shifting resources only when the price system proves inadequate. We have stated earlier that large and rapid changes cannot be carried out well by the methods that serve to guide economic activity in peacetime.

We are now ready to show why this statement is true by tracing some of the effects of the early steps in defense mobilization.

In the peacetime economy, Government buys a considerable part of the output of some private firms to construct bridges, dams, and other public works, and to equip and supply the standing Army, Navy, and Air Force. Such Government purchases amount to only a small part of the total business done by most firms in the country, but they create the channels through which the first steps toward mobilization are taken. In other words, as mobilization begins, Government starts to work through the price system into which its peacetime operations are geared.

Building Defense Capacity

Working through already existing channels, Government can begin to build up defense capacity in either of two ways: It may order plant and equipment from firms, or it may order goods the production of which will require the purchase of plant and equipment by the firms themselves. In either event, the result is that new productive capacity for defense is created.

The purchase of equipment and the procurement of supplies by the various Government agencies and by the armed forces involve many complications of organization and procedure. Since we are not concerned with any of these, we shall continue to speak simply of "Government" as doing the buying, and leave the details to those interested in them. In very general terms, Government purchasing from firms may be broken into three steps:

1. *Appropriations.* When Government agencies propose

to spend money, their plans must be submitted to Congress, and bills must be written and passed embodying the appropriations. At this stage of the process, the views of the public get a hearing in Congressional debate, and the sums of money requested are not always to be had. Bills providing for defense capacity, however, are ordinarily passed, and the plans of Government are not severely hampered by lack of appropriations.

2. *Contracts.* The second step is to negotiate contracts between Government and private firms. Government in peacetime makes some important purchases in the open market; more often, Government agencies state their requirements, and accept the best offer made by firms, or arrange to have products made to order.

In getting defense capacity built up, Government relies mainly on special contracts made with the particular firms that seem best able to meet its needs. These firms are likely to be large corporations, and objections are frequently made to the effect that Government favors the large at the expense of the smaller concerns. Without necessarily approving the Government's procedure, let us try to account for it.

To begin with, contracts with Government are not so eagerly sought as one might suppose, for Government makes altogether too many special stipulations to suit most firms. Furthermore, large firms do, in fact, pass on much of their Government business to other smaller firms by making sub-contracts with them. Finally, Government contracts with large firms make maximum use of existing arrangements, and avoid much wasteful duplication of effort by fixing responsibility in one place. When Government makes a contract with General Motors, for instance, the existing organization within the corporation is being used to control all the details of production, and this one firm is held wholly responsible for the result. All subcontracts made are at the discretion of the corporation, and Government has to concern itself with none of them. If Government were to go directly to the smaller firms, it would itself have to undertake all the co-ordinating functions that General Motors is already equipped to perform.

Whether these considerations are or are not sufficient to justify the action of Government is a debatable question. At any rate, there is little doubt as to why Government acts as it does.

3. *Payments.* Most Government purchases are paid for on delivery. If a completely equipped factory is being bought, Government may pay for it in a number of stages as various steps in construction are taken. On the whole, however, firms get little money from Government until after production has taken place. When Government is contracting for goods that require a firm to provide its own special plant and equipment, Government may never pay for the new plant as such. The plant may be paid for indirectly, if Government agencies continue to buy the products turned out, or special tax concessions may be made to help firms recover their outlays. The point to be emphasized is that firms must nearly always finance their own defense production first, and collect from Government afterward. Where do firms get the money they need, and where does Government get the money to make the final payments?

Financing Mobilization

Firms finance defense production much as they finance increases in peacetime production. They may have some idle funds of their own to invest, and they may raise new capital by selling securities to households. To a very large extent, however, firms borrow from commercial banks to get the money for increased payrolls, more raw materials, and so on.

We shall have occasion to examine the banking system in some detail when we take up the question of indirect Government controls in Chapter 7. Meanwhile, the reader who is following this discussion with the aid of a sketch of Figure 4.1 may wish to add a small area labelled "banks" at any convenient point outside the circular flow, and draw connecting lines from the new area to firms and Government. With this slight modification, the model will reveal very clearly the effects to be considered, and the relevant flows may even be incorporated in the rough diagram. Readers who are interested in the model technique itself will observe one of its peculiarities: Effects stand out much more clearly as they are being inserted one by one than they do afterward. Drawing rough sketches and tracing relationships is far more enlightening than inspecting the results.

Returning to the financing of defense production by banks, we may first observe that firms holding Government contracts are excellent credit risks, since there is little doubt about their ability to repay loans. When such firms go to commercial banks, they sign promissory notes for the money they need, and the banks advance this money in the form of deposit accounts on which the firms can write checks. As the firms increase production, they write checks on their new deposits to pay additional employes and buy more raw materials, and the people who receive these checks either cash them or deposit them in their own bank accounts. As defense capacity expands, then, a flow of new money enters the income stream, raising the level of the stream as it moves from firms to households through the Market for Productive Services. So far, increases in production have the same effects on household income as in peacetime.

In the peacetime economy, firms as a group ordinarily pay off their bank loans out of the money they get by selling more goods to consumers, and as the loans are repaid the level of income tends to fall just as it rose before. In the defense economy, however, firms pay off their loans not out of consumer spending but out of the money they get from Government as contracts are fulfilled. As our model shows, what happens to the level of income depends on the source of the funds that Government spends.

Government finances its defense expenditures by taxing and by borrowing. Most of the money that Government collects in taxes comes out of the current income stream, so to the extent that firms are paid from this source the level of income tends to fall as in peacetime. Taxes flow from firms and households to Government, out of the Government area to that of defense capacity, and finally out of that area and into the banks.

When Government borrows by selling bonds to firms and households, the money that flows through the Government area to defense capacity and into the banks comes out of the income stream only in part. If firms and households reduce their other expenditures on purpose to buy the bonds, the level of income is lowered to that extent. Usually, however, much of the money with which firms and households buy Government bonds is money they were already holding out of the income stream in idle bank deposits, and as this money was not circulating anyway the level of income is not reduced by the Government borrowing.

Finally, the money that Government borrows by selling bonds to banks is drawn entirely from outside the income stream. In so far as defense mobilization is financed in this way we have a steady flow of new funds into the income stream, and the level of income tends to keep rising. Looking at our model, we can visualize the process as a whole, and observe its effects on the flow of income. *First,* we have firms with defense contracts borrowing at the banks, and injecting new money into the circular flow as production increases. *Second,* we have firms repaying their bank loans as they turn over their output to Government. *Third,* we have Government borrowing from the banks to pay the firms that are paying the banks. The net result, then, is the creation of a steady stream of payments from banks to Government to firms and back again to banks in addition to the flow from banks to defense firms that swells the income stream. To the extent that Government finances mobilization by selling bonds to banks, all the money spent in building defense capacity becomes increased income that households may use as they wish.

Mobilization and the Price System

We are now in a position to observe the effects of mobilization on the price system, and to see what problems arise as a result.

As we look at our model, we can think of the prices existing in the Market for Productive Services at any given time as the results of bargaining between firms and households as firms buy the labor and resources being used in current production. The various prices being paid by firms and received by households in this market are channelling all the different types of labor and resources into the production of the goods being made by the firms.

As mobilization begins, Government makes use of the price system to shift labor and resources from current uses into defense production, and to attract a larger total flow of productive services from households to the market. At first, this may be done very easily. All Government needs to do is to offer defense contracts to firms at high enough prices to make the building of defense capacity more profitable than civilian production. Firms with Government contracts can then borrow at banks, and by offering somewhat higher prices for the particular productive services they want can both divert these services from other firms to themselves, and stimulate an increased flow to the market. At the outset, then, the price system functions as in peacetime, and Government has to take no extraordinary steps to get the output it needs.

As mobilization proceeds, however, the situation deteriorates very rapidly. As we have already seen in our model, the building of defense capacity raises household income immediately, and in the absence of other influences, households will increase their expenditures in the Market for Consumer Goods. Prices in this market start to rise, and firms can then increase their profits as in peacetime by producing more consumer goods. Consequently, firms producing civilian goods will expand their purchases of productive services in competition with the firms working on Government contracts. But this is exactly what civilian goods firms must not be permitted to do. Labor and resources are supposed to move away from civilian goods firms rather than toward them, and any additional productive services that households may supply are supposed to be absorbed in the building of defense capacity.

As soon as Government begins to use the price system to shift labor and resources, the system begins to defeat this purpose. If Government should insist in continuing as it began, it could keep on shifting resources only by paying higher and higher prices for them. Meanwhile, there would be a steady drain of resources into civilian production, for the more the money that Government spent, the more the rise of consumer goods' prices, and the more the inducement of firms to increase civilian output.

The price system does not serve well to effect large changes, because large changes produce large reactions in the price system itself. This is just as true in peacetime as in the defense economy, but the operations of a single firm or household are seldom on a large enough scale to affect the price system as a whole materially. Occasionally, to be sure, some large firm may try to produce a new product, and discover that its own demand for specialized material and skilled labor raises the prices of these essentials so much that the whole project must be abandoned as unprofitable. Occurrences of this sort are mere incidents in the operation of the peacetime economy, but Government projects in the defense economy cannot be abandoned, and they must not be permitted to fail.

Before going on, let us pause a moment to dispose of a false lead that appears to hold some promise, but that really gets us nowhere. At first glance, it appears from our model that Government could continue to work entirely through the price system if it could cut off the flow of increased spending from households to the Market for Consumer Goods. It is this extra spending that raises consumer goods' prices and provides the incentive for civilian producers to increase output. If Government were to levy such heavy taxes on households that all their increased income were taken away from them, it might seem that the problem would be solved at once. Actually, this would be no solution.

The higher prices that Government offers firms, and that firms in turn pay households for productive services, provide the stimulus to households to offer more of their services for use in defense production. As wages rise, for example, part-time workers, married women, and many others who do not customarily work for pay, begin to appear in defense plants. It is the higher prices, and the increased sale of their services at these higher prices that give many households larger incomes. Now, what becomes of the incentives if the increased incomes are taxed away? In an effort to maintain former standards, some people, no doubt, will work harder and for longer hours when their incomes are shrinking. If such people could be identified, special incentives might be designed for them, but for most of us the lure of increased income seems to be more effective. So far as this incentive is concerned it clearly will not do to raise incomes with the understanding that all the increases will be taxed away. We should observe, moreover, that a solution is not to be found in the taxing by Government of other households, whose incomes have not increased, with a view to making total taxes equal total defense expenditures. What this would do would be to take money from people who would not have spent more anyway, leaving others to do the increased spending.

Bottlenecks and Inflation

Our discussion of the initial phase of shifting resources by means of the price system may be completed by calling attention to two special problems:

1. *Bottlenecks.* Bottlenecks in production arise whenever there are too few resources of a particular type or workers having some special skill to fill all existing requirements. In the peacetime economy such bottlenecks often exist, and they give rise to extraordinarily high prices for these special productive services. The high prices in turn lead to a gradual increase in the total quantities of such services flowing to the market. In a building boom, for instance, there may be an unusually great demand for skilled carpenters to do the finish work on houses. The wages of such carpenters will rise to high levels, and if the demand continues over some years, more men will take the time and trouble to learn the required skills, and the number of finish carpenters will slowly increase. Meanwhile, builders must make out as best they can, and many of them will have to put up with inferior work.

In the defense economy, bottlenecks are a serious matter, for Government can neither do without specialized labor and resources nor wait very long for the total flow to the market to increase. It is possible that defense projects might require more skilled workers, say, than existed in the entire country, but it is much more likely that the skilled workers wanted are already employed elsewhere, and that they are satisfied not only with their incomes but with their homes and community lives as well. Offering such people higher wages will not get them to move half-way across the continent to take temporary jobs in defense production, and those who move at all will move reluctantly. In brief, our earlier generalization is borne out again: The price system does not function satisfactorily to accomplish changes that must be made quickly and on a large scale. When bottlenecks develop in the defense economy, Government must find some means of breaking them immediately, and direct action will supplant the price system.

2. *Inflation.* Inflation not merely increases the immediate difficulties of mobilization, but gives rise to so many serious problems that it justifies treatment as a separate aspect of the whole defense economy. To complete the present discussion, therefore, we shall merely repeat that Government cannot conduct defense mobilization wholly through the price system and prevent inflation at the same time. An inflationary gap appears as soon as Government tries to use the price system to build defense capacity, and Government must take special action to prevent competition with itself, if for no other reason.

Chapter 6

INFLATION

Many books have been written about the nature, causes, and consequences of inflation, and many more will doubtless be written in years to come. Since inflation affects everyone in the economy, it is only natural that there should be widespread interest in the subject, and that discussion should reveal numerous differences of opinion.

So far as the existence of inflation at any given time is concerned, most of the arguments have to do with matters of definition. Some people think of any price rise at all as inflationary. Others prefer to speak of inflation only when price increases are large and rapid. Still others believe that inflation should be defined in terms of its causes. Thus, inflation would be said to exist only if price increases were brought about by an increase in the quantity of money in circulation, by extraordinary Government spending, by overissue of paper currency, and so on. Since each particular cause must itself be defined and explained, it is easy to see that we shall get nowhere in our own treatment of inflation until we have agreed on the use of the term.

The Meaning of Inflation

For the purpose of the present discussion, we shall define inflation as an increase in the price level of consumer goods, regardless of its basic cause or ultimate extent. Even small and short-lived price increases are included in the definition, but the major movements are naturally the ones to stress.

The immediate cause of inflation, as we have defined it, is invariably the same. Let us look at the Market for Consumer Goods in any of our models. In this market, a stream of household expenditure meets a stream of output flowing from firms, and the price level of consumer goods is the ratio between the number of dollars spent and the number of units of output changing hands. If $100 is spent on 100 units, for instance, the average price per unit is $1. Some units cost more than $1 and others cost less, but consumers must be paying $1 on the average for each pound, pint, or piece of merchandise they buy. If more than $100 were to be spent on the same 100 units of output, the average of prices would rise to more than $1, and this increase in the price level would be inflation.

As we are using the term, inflation must always mean an increase in expenditure relative to amounts sold. Let us now see what brings this about.

Causes of Inflation

In the peacetime economy inflation is a characteristic feature of periods of prosperity. As we know, investment then creates a great deal of household income in addition to what people earn in the production of consumer goods, and as households begin to spend more money the price level of consumer goods begins to rise. In peacetime this sort of inflation tends to die a natural death. The rising prices of consumer goods induce firms to expand the production of these goods considerably, and the investment that is raising household income is creating new productive capacity that will shortly increase the output of consumer goods still more. Meanwhile, households are increasing their saving as well as their spending. When investment begins to slacken, saving soon overtakes it, and households withdraw as much money from the income stream as firms are injecting.

Inflation in the peacetime economy is simply one aspect of the regular operation of the price system. It gives rise to no extraordinary problems, and few people worry much about it. The cause of peacetime inflation is seen to be increased consumer spending out of the increased household income created by investment. When investment is rapidly increasing, total production and hence total income expands faster than the production of consumer goods. When investment tapers off, the output of consumer goods increases faster than production as a whole, and inflation is checked automatically.

Let us next look briefly at war inflation. In our model of the war economy, we observe that war inflation begins in much the same way as peacetime inflation, with total output rising faster than the output of consumer goods alone. As household income and spending increase faster than the flow of consumer goods to the market, prices start to rise. War inflation, however, is not self-limiting in the same way as peacetime inflation. Increases in production are increases in war production, and not investment in new capacity to produce consumer goods. As the price level of consumer goods rises, there is no increased production of these goods, either immediately or after some time. On the contrary, it is likely that the production of consumer goods will be rapidly reduced, and more and more of total output taken by Government to be destroyed in the war. Unless strong measures are invoked, war inflation can therefore carry prices to extremely high levels.

In the defense economy, inflation tends to develop as in the war economy, though on a smaller scale. As defense capacity is built up, the increased production generates increased household income, while the output of consumer goods fails to expand. Households have more money to spend on the same flow of output and prices begin to rise in the Market for Consumer Goods.

The Mechanism of Inflation

We may now look more carefully into the process of inflation in order to see how inflation, once started, develops momentum that tends to raise prices higher and higher as time goes on. The essential nature of the process may be displayed in a simplified model of the economy, in which all efforts of Government to check inflation are disregarded. In Figure 6.1 we have such a model containing only firms, households, and the two markets through which they deal with one another. We suppose that firms are injecting new money into the income stream to increase productive capacity for peace or war, and that the source of the new money is somewhere outside the existing income stream itself. With the aid of a few imaginary figures, we may examine the inflationary mechanism.

If the reader is sketching the diagrams as they are introduced, he may wish to write the assumed figures into his sketch at the relevant points. While this is not essential to an understanding of the present analysis, it should make the discussion easier to follow, since it has been written with a view to this sort of application.

INFLATION

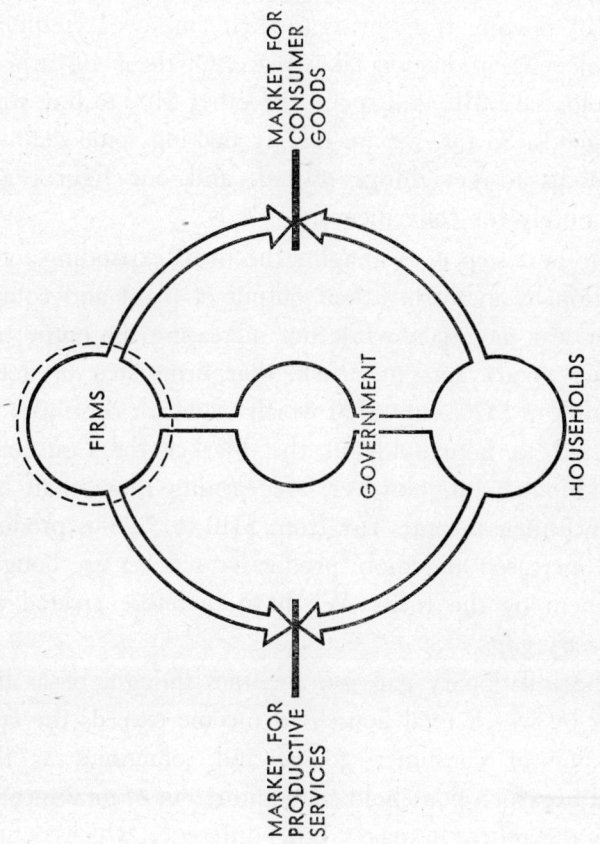

Figure 6.1. THE SIMPLIFIED MODEL.

1. Let us begin by supposing that total production is valued at $110, of which $100 is consumer goods and the other $10 new productive capacity. Household income is thus $110, flowing from firms to their employes, creditors, and owners as production takes place. Of the $110 earned, households save $10, and spend the other $100 to buy consumer goods. So far, we are merely making some definite assumptions to get things started, and our figures are chosen purely for convenience.

2. The next step is to imagine the firms expanding total production by increasing their output of plant and equipment or war materials, while not increasing the output of consumer goods. Imagine, then, that firms step up total production to $120, only $100 worth of which continues to be offered to households in the Market for Consumer Goods. Households, however, are earning more than before, since their incomes rise from $110 to $120 as production in increased and more productive services are bought from them by the firms. We have therefore created an *inflationary gap*.

3. The inflationary gap is sometimes thought of as the amount by which total household income exceeds the current value of consumer goods, and sometimes as the amount by which household expenditure out of total income exceeds the other. It makes little difference which definition we use, as long as we stick to one or the other consistently. Let us agree, then, to speak of the inflationary gap as the excess money that consumers will spend over and above the value of consumer goods at existing prices. If total household income rises by $10, households may want to save some part of the increase; say half. The other

half gives us an inflationary gap of $5. What happens next?

4. The inflationary gap is closed as soon as households spend $105 to buy $100 worth of consumer goods. Prices rise enough to make all the goods put together sell for $105 instead of $100, and we have the first evidence of inflation in the system. So far, everything is obvious enough, but what we want to know is why the inflationary gap does not stay closed. After prices have risen once, why should they rise again and again? In other words, what is the inflationary mechanism?

5. A good way to reveal the nature of the inflationary mechanism is to see how quickly inflation comes to an end when the mechanism does not function. Let us imagine, then, that after the inflationary gap has been closed by the first price increases, firms produce in the same way as before. The consumer goods they turn out are valued at $105 rather than $100, but defense or other additional output is still $20. As we can easily see in our model, total household income becomes $105 plus the $20, instead of $100 plus the $20 as formerly. The members of the economy as employes, creditors, and owners of firms are naturally earning what they are spending as households plus whatever other spending is done to produce non-consumer goods.

With total income of $125, households will wish to save part of the extra $5, and spend the rest on consumer goods. If the division is again half and half, we have a new inflationary gap of $2.50, which may be closed by a second price increase. If firms repeat their $20 of extra production, total household income will now be up by this $2.50, half of which may again be added to spending on consumer goods. If the process is repeated, however, the increase in income will be but $1.25 next time, and on each successive round it gets smaller and smaller until it has become negligible. In other words, the inflationary gap grows smaller and smaller as time goes on, and tends soon to vanish altogether. Inflation thus dies out quickly when households are not getting increases in income from some source other than their own increases in spending.

This same effect may also be visualized in terms of the saving-investment relationships developed in Chapter 2. If investment or other equivalent spending fails to increase from round to round of the circular flow, income will increase only until saving out of the rising income equals the current volume of investment. Income can then rise no more, and household spending on consumer goods will stop increasing, with inflation coming to an end.

6. Eliminating the mechanism that produces sustained inflation from our picture enables us to identify it readily. To open an inflationary gap and keep it open continually, the income stream must be fed by increasingly large sums of money spent in producing something besides consumer goods. In the peacetime economy, this will be money invested in new plant and equipment, and the inflationary gap will open and close as prosperity rises toward its peak, and recession succeeds it.

When business prospects begin to improve after a peacetime depression, firms take advantage of new profit opportunities that arise from the progress of invention, the discovery of new resources, and so on, and begin to invest in additional plant and equipment. Total investment at first is comparatively small, but since it generates increased income and consumer spending, it stimulates further investment as time goes on. Each time that consumers spend more money, firms inject a larger sum into the income stream than on the previous round. As investment spending continues to grow, the inflationary gap is thus kept open, and prices rise during the period of prosperity. When enough projects have been completed to check the growth in size of the investment injections from one round to the next, only consumer spending remains to keep income rising, and the inflationary gap soon disappears.

Leaving details to one side, we thus observe that sustained inflation requires a continual increase in the sums spent by firms in producing other than consumer goods. Unless the firms inject larger and larger sums of money from round to round, saving will overtake investment as income rises, and the inflationary gap will accordingly vanish.

7. In the war economy, the inflationary gap is kept open by the increasing amounts of money spent by Government on war production. If the war should last long enough, the amount added by Government to income on each round of spending would presumably reach some maximum and stop increasing. Inflation, however, would be violent long before such a final check could operate, especially since the output of consumer goods would be tending to decrease as the war was fought.

8. In the defense economy, the inflationary gap is kept open much as in wartime. Mobilization at first moves slowly, and spending on defense capacity is comparatively small. As plans are made and put into operation, the pace becomes more rapid, and defense capacity is built up faster and faster. Beyond the early phases, however, it is less easy

to generalize. The fact that the speed of mobilization cannot be fixed in advance means that the spending on defense capacity will not necessarily increase up to some peak, and then level off or decline. Instead, it is probable that the rate of mobilization will be irregular, with ups and downs in spending that are unpredictable. Defense inflation may thus be characterized as follows:

Over the period of mobilization as a whole, an inflationary gap tends to be created by the building of defense capacity. In the long run, inflation is therefore bound to occur unless the strongest measures are taken to control it. From time to time, however, there is some slowing down of mobilization, and some increase in the output of consumer goods. Inflation is thus an irregular movement, with rapid price advances followed by movements sideways or even slightly downward before further advances occur.

The Cost-Price Spiral

Sustained inflation, as we have just seen, requires that at each round of the circular flow firms increase the size of their expenditures on the production of non-consumer goods. This general mechanism of inflation tends to operate in peacetime prosperities, and in a war or defense economy as well. A special feature of the mechanism has not, however, been mentioned. This aspect of inflation is known as the "cost-price spiral." Let us continue to refer to our simplified model, and see how this spiral works.

Looking at the Market for Productive Services, we observe that the increases in income created by increases in non-consumption output are reaching households as they sell their labor services and resources to firms. When production begins to expand, households may be ready to supply more productive services at the existing prices, especially if there is considerable unemployment at the outset. But as firms go on increasing output, they soon discover that the flow of additional services from households to the market is drying up, and that more will continue to be forthcoming only if higher prices are paid for them. As the total flow begins to level off, moreover, firms must compete more actively with one another for the limited quantities to be had. This competition naturally takes the form of offers of higher pay and better terms than those currently existing in the market. Thus, as the prices of productive services rise, firms must spend more money to buy any given number of these services, and more income tends to be created on each round, even if physical output increases little or none. Since the prices of consumer goods keep rising, people must get more income to live as well as before, and in selling productive services to firms households therefore drive as hard bargains as they can.

Now, as costs of production increase, firms raise their selling prices to cover the higher costs, and we have another aspect of inflation. Firms raise prices, not merely because they find that households are increasing demand in the Market for Consumer Goods, but also because prices must go up if profit margins are to be maintained. As goods pass from one firm to another on their way to consumers, there is a magnified effect through the mark-up system.

Let us imagine that the area containing firms in our simplified model is divided into a number of sectors by vertical lines drawn across it. To save trouble, we may settle for two lines that will give us three sectors in the whole area. We now suppose that the sector nearest the Market for Consumer Goods contains retailers; the middle sector, wholesalers; and the sector nearest the Market for Productive Services, manufacturers.

As goods move from manufacturers to wholesalers, from wholesalers to retailers, and from retailers to consumers, a price mark-up takes place at each step in the journey. Business practices vary, of course, from one trade to another; we are interested in only the general effect. If a wholesaler adds, say, a 20% mark-up to the price he pays the manufacturer, the manufacturer's price plus this mark-up becomes the cost of goods bought by the retailer. The retailer may then add 40% as his mark-up, and the wholesale price plus this mark-up becomes the price to consumers. A mark-up of 20% or 40% is not to be confused with a rate of profit, since all costs of doing business have to come out of the mark-up before profits are made. A retailer, for instance, can be pricing his goods on a 100% mark-up, and still be unable to break even.

Apart from the question of profit or loss, the point to observe is that the mark-ups at each stage of production and sale are a percentage of the cost to the seller. It can hardly be news to anyone that mark-ups bear some relation to the cost of goods, and that an automobile is marked up by more dollars than is a loaf of bread. The relation between mark-ups and inflation, however, is more likely to escape notice.

Suppose, for example, that a manufacturer grants an increase in wage rates, and that his total cost per unit of output is thereby raised from $100 to $110. If the manufacturer adds a 20% mark-up in selling to wholesalers, the cost to wholesalers is increased from the previous $120 to $132. This is $2 more than the increase in the manufacturer's cost. As the wholesaler adds his 20% mark-up to the $132 instead of the $120, the cost to retailers rises from $144 to $158. In other words, retailers pay $14 more than previously, which is $4 over and above the initial cost increase. By the time the retailer had added his own 40% mark-up, consumers are going to have to pay a price that has risen by roughly twice the increase in manufacturing cost. Although this illustration assumes particular values that are no more typical than others that might have been chosen, it is clear that the overall tendency of mark-ups is to magnify cost increases into greater increases in the prices of consumer goods. This fact largely accounts for the increasing profits that firms in general make during periods of inflation; it also explains the strength of the cost-price spiral. The prices of consumer goods rise faster than the wages and other payments to households that make up production costs, and households find their incomes increasing more slowly than the cost of living.

Before leaving the subject of the cost-price spiral, let us try to see a little more clearly how the spiral is related to inflation. Does the cost-price spiral itself cause inflation? Does it aggravate inflation produced by other causes? Or, is it simply one of the details of the inflationary process without independent significance? Let us test the possibilities with the aid of our simplified model.

If the cost-price spiral is an independent force capable of producing inflation in the absence of other causes, our model should be able to establish the fact. We must assume to begin with that everything in the model is running along smoothly, with no inflationary gap due to other factors. Our cost-price spiral must not get under way with an initial rise in the prices of consumer goods, for this is what the spiral itself is supposed to produce. We must therefore start with an increase in production costs, and since the "wage-price spiral" is most often referred to, we shall suppose that strong labor unions demand and get higher wages. Production costs are thus increased, and the firms affected mark up their selling prices, with further mark-ups following all along the line. Prices to consumers are up by more dollars than the original increase in costs, and inflation seems about to begin. At this point, however, a difficulty emerges. If prices are raised, who is going to pay them? The only households that have extra income are those that got the wage increases, and since the wage increases amount to less money than the price increases, these households are not getting enough more dollars to buy the goods. Furthermore, to the extent that the households with higher incomes choose to save part of the increase, the shortage of purchasing power is even greater.

In order to clear the Market for Consumer Goods of all the products offered at the higher level of prices, households as a group would have to spend all the increased income from the higher wages plus enough to cover the amounts added to retail prices by all the mark-ups that have occurred. If all the households put together should start to save less of their current income, and spend more on consumer goods, the deficit could be covered. Otherwise, the market could not be cleared unless prices were cut, or output reduced, or both. But, why should households decide to cut their saving at just the proper moment? Such a neat and spontaneous adjustment is, of course, conceivable, but it seems scarcely probable. We therefore conclude that the cost-price spiral is unlikely to be the original cause of inflation.

This finding may be further strengthened by returning for a moment to the wage increase with which the spiral was supposed to begin. As soon as we ask ourselves on just what grounds the higher wages were demanded and granted, we realize that the question cannot be readily answered. Unions are not quite so likely to demand wage increases in otherwise stable situations as might be imagined. If we simply assume that the increase is demanded out of a clear sky, we must still explain how it can be granted, and especially how firms propose to pass it on in higher price quotations. What can give management good reason to believe that higher prices are going to be paid? To get much of a cost-price spiral started, we must clearly presuppose conditions not of general economic depression or even of stability, but rather of some inflation already in progress.

If an inflationary gap is presupposed, the cost-price spiral is easy to account for. With the prices of consumer goods already rising, wage increases will be demanded on the ground of higher costs of living. Indeed, a good many union contracts contain "escalator" clauses that provide for automatic pay increases if the cost of living goes up. Firms raise wages, and pass the cost increases along with confidence that higher prices will not hurt their business.

Has the cost-price spiral, then, no independent significance? So far, we have been looking at it from the standpoint of total income, total spending, and the average prices of all consumer goods taken together. From this point of view, we may say that its independent influence as a cause of general inflation is negligible. More searching analysis might suggest some qualifications to this conclusion, but it seems probable that the significance of the cost-price spiral is to be sought within a general inflationary movement the origins of which lie elsewhere. Let us see just what this means.

As soon as we begin to think in terms of individuals rather than of groups, we recognize that the picture of wage earners spending much of their income on the particular products they help produce is not very realistic. Most Ford employes may drive Ford cars, for instance, but even if all of them did, they would still spend most of their earnings on other things. When the Ford Motor Company grants a pay increase, management has no notion of recovering the extra money by selling at higher prices to Ford workers. Other people are expected to pay the higher prices, while the higher wages are spent on the products of quite different firms. These familiar facts suggest that the cost-price spiral may play a part in creating specific inflationary gaps within the inflationary gap as a whole, and possibilities at once come to mind.

What do wage earners ordinarily do with increases in pay? They may increase their saving, but they also increase their spending, and one of the things they spend more money on is food. Not that they eat much more; they eat food of better quality that costs more money. Since food is a large element in the cost of living, increases in the price of food lead to demands for higher wages, so a special wage-price spiral can exist. Furthermore, the production of increased quantities of food takes a comparatively long time, for crops must be planted, livestock grown, and so on. The wage-food-price spiral may thus lead a life partly of its own, with higher wages being followed by more spending on food, rising food prices, and again higher wages to compensate for the higher cost of living. Meanwhile, the higher wage costs of firms are reflected in higher prices of other goods.

Other special cost-price spirals exist, but the one we have mentioned is among the most important. It creates a special problem for Government to deal with during defense mobilization, and it will be referred to again in connection with controls. At present we should observe that a special spiral, like an overall spiral, can function on a serious scale only if some general inflation is already present. Wage increases cannot be passed along in price increases unless households as a group are increasing their expenditures.

Consequences of Inflation

In order to see why inflation is so generally feared, and why Government tries to prevent or control it, let us suppose that all limitations are absent, and that inflation continues unchecked. What are the consequences of unrestrained inflation?

Since we are interested primarily in the defense economy, let us relate our discussion to that model in particular. We already know roughly what inflation amounts to in a peacetime economy, and war inflation is similar to defense inflation, only more so. The effects of inflation may be reduced to a single statement: Inflation alters price relationships, and unrestrained inflation distorts the whole price system. Let us try to see concretely what this implies.

The inflations that accompany prosperities in the peacetime economy are comparatively short and mild, and the changing price relationships that take place perform important functions as we know. The rising prices of consumer goods call forth more production of these goods; changing prices of productive services shift labor and resources from old uses into new; and households offer larger total quantities of productive services as their prices rise. In the defense economy, the first of these reactions is, of course, not wanted, and Government may short cut the price system in order to prevent it. At the moment, however, the thing to notice is that the price system performs its peacetime functions tolerably well because price changes serve as guides to action by households and firms.

When price changes are small and gradual, people can make sensible plans for the near future, for they can calculate roughly what will be to their advantage in terms of price relationships. Firms can plan what to produce and how much; households can plan their saving and spending; Government agencies can estimate their costs, and appropriations can be intelligently made. If prices are rising rapidly, and the relationships among the prices of various things are being radically altered, the price system loses much of its co-ordinating power.

Looking at our model, let us begin with the Market for Productive Services. As inflation proceeds, the prices of all these services are tending to rise, but different prices rise at very different rates of speed. The prices of many services are fixed for long periods by contracts between households and firms. Salaries, for example, are agreed upon as a certain amount each year, with the sum frequently fixed for several years in advance. Firms that have borrowed from households by selling them bonds have agreed to pay a definite number of dollars a year as interest until the bonds fall due, and this may be a half-century later. Leases fixing the rent of land and buildings, pensions and annuities, dividends on preferred stock, royalties, and many other contractual arrangements are similarly made to cover extended periods. Even wages are likely to be fixed for a year at a time by contracts between unions and employers. Wage contracts may contain escalator clauses providing for wage increases if the cost of living rises, but this does not mean daily or weekly wage adjustments. To some extent, escalator clauses may even keep wages from rising as far as they otherwise might, since cost of living increases take place at only the agreed upon intervals.

Now, as firms begin to compete with one another for additional productive services, prices in this market rise very unevenly. Price increases tend to be greatest in those parts of the market where scarcities are greatest, and where prices are fixed for the shortest periods by existing contracts. Scarcity must naturally be thought of as a shortage relative to demand; there is no shortage of idiots though their numbers are limited. Particular types of skilled labor and specialized resources become scarce when firms want more than can be had, and bid against one another for the inadequate total. When such bottlenecks develop, the prices of these productive services rise very rapidly without yielding an increased flow to the market, and largely without shifting the existing flow into the most essential uses. In the defense economy, civilian goods firms that already have the skilled workers they need may keep raising their pay, thus preventing their moving to defense production.

Looking next at the firms in our model, we may see from their position between the two markets how inflation affects them. Since, in general, the prices of consumer goods rise faster than the prices of productive services, firms as a group make larger and larger profits as inflation proceeds. The largest gains go to those firms that are best protected against increases in competition in both markets, for the prices of their products will rise most rapidly, while their costs are rising most slowly. Firms that hold such resources as mines, forests, oil wells, and real estate are among the major beneficiaries, which explains why rent control is likely to be undertaken in a war or defense economy.

Farmers as a group tend to gain substantially from inflation. Farming is usually regarded as a highly competitive business, but as we have remarked, it is protection against *increases* in competition that counts, and in this respect farmers are in a favorable position. As household income rises, one of the major demands is for more and better food. Food prices start to rise, but total food production cannot be increased very fast, and all farmers put together take in more and more money for comparatively little more output. Furthermore, there is no great increase in the number of farmers, for few people can take up farming on short notice. Costs of farm production naturally rise with the prices of productive services, but farmers who own their farms or have long-term leases are largely protected here. Short-term renters and share-croppers have to turn over part of their gains to land owners.

Since inflation creates larger profits, it might seem as if most businessmen ought to favor inflation on the largest possible scale. Many farmers do, in fact, want a good deal of inflation, for they regard it as a means of recovering some of the losses they have suffered during much of the present century. Even farmers, however, would hardly care to see inflation go on indefinitely, and most other businessmen would be satisfied with little or none.

Opposition to mild inflation is due mainly to the fear that it will not be stopped in time, or that it will be halted by extreme measures on the part of Government. Opposition to violent inflation, however, is due to the disastrous effects it produces on business enterprise itself. As prices keep rising, and as different costs keep rising at different rates, businessmen find it impossible to calculate what their expenses will be even a short time ahead. Consider, for instance, a firm that has been making large inflationary profits, and that then finds it necessary to replace a lot of its old plant and equipment. The prices of the things it needs may suddenly take a spurt that will not only wipe out all the gains made so far, but will cost more money besides. Inflationary bottlenecks in labor and materials may make it impossible to carry on regular operations, and rapid increases in wages paid elsewhere may make it hard to keep a working force together. As the prices of productive services keep rising, households begin to anticipate further increases, and become reluctant to commit themselves to long-term contracts with firms. Some firms actually find that they can advantageously stop producing altogether, and simply buy scarce resources to sell to others at the higher prices inflation will bring. Inflation on a large scale, then, disorganizes production, and may result in a decrease in total output. Needless to say, these effects make inflation still more rapid, and further magnify the consequences.

Let us consider finally the effects of inflation on the households in our model. As the prices of consumer goods rise, money loses its value to households, since each dollar will buy less and less as time goes on. Total household income, on the other hand, keeps increasing, so the shrinking value of the dollar is partly offset by the larger number of dollars in the income stream. Notice, however, the consequences to saving.

In the peacetime economy, households get ahead in the world and prepare themselves for emergencies by saving part of their income, depositing the money in savings banks, buying bonds with it, and so on. For most households, saving represents a sacrifice of consumer goods that might otherwise have been bought and enjoyed, and we think of the value of our savings in terms of what the money would buy. As inflation continues, the total saved over a lifetime will buy less and less, and in a really violent inflation the value of all the past savings of households may be virtually wiped out. Furthermore, nobody has any idea how much money it will take to buy any given thing in the future, so the safest thing to do with current income is to save none of it, but to spend it all immediately. Pensions, and annuities acquired at great sacrifice become worthless. Families are unable to plan for their children's education, for illness, or for other contingencies. Life insurance policies lose their appeal to people of ordinary intelligence. In brief, all the arrangements that households count upon to provide some measure of security in an uncertain world become valueless if inflation is unchecked.

Since inflation involves a violent distortion of the price system that destroys much of the basis for ordinary business and family life, we are likely to get the impression that it leads to economic disaster for everyone. This is by no means true. Unrestrained inflation produces a wholesale and sudden shift in income distribution; many are ruined, but others prosper. As we should expect, it is on the whole the people who have been faring best under the price system who lose the most when the system changes. Families with fortunes invested in gilt-edged bonds can barely survive, and conservative businessmen go bankrupt. At the same time, speculators, gamblers, black market operators, and racketeers grow rich.

The gains are not wholly confined to the wicked. Farmers, as we have seen, tend to prosper during inflation, and anyone whose income rises faster than the cost of living may find his lot improving. When some are gaining at the expense of others, however, it is those who are doing so most obviously who create the most trouble. Since the really spectacular gains tend to go to people who are hardly thought of as public benefactors anyway, inflation is a serious threat to national morale. Unrestrained inflation clearly will not do in a defense economy, when co-operation and collective action are essential to get results.

Inflation in the Defense Economy

Although inflation cannot be permitted to develop to large proportions during mobilization, mild inflation would appear to be tolerable and even desirable.

To begin with, slowly rising prices do little of the damage that is done by violent inflation, for the reason that everyone has time to get used to the changes while they are occurring. Mild inflation is exactly what we are accustomed to during peacetime prosperities; it is the normal accompaniment of growth in productive capacity, and we are all thoroughly familiar with it. To insist that there should be no inflation whatever during defense mobilization is to insist on radical changes involving direct action by Government.

Gradual inflation has the important advantage of reducing the burden that falls on households when the output of consumer goods fails to increase or is actually reduced. Since households cannot buy any more consumer goods than there are to be had, it has sometimes been said that they should be made clearly aware of this fact by taking away from them all the increases in money income that lead to inflation. If consumers cannot buy more goods, why let them think so? Why let them have more money just to bid up the prices of the things they can still get?

The answer to this question is that no household can tell just how much real income is being lost through price increases, if its money income keeps rising all the time. The notion that because some sacrifices are necessary people must be made to realize how large their sacrifices are is like arguing that no one should take an anaesthetic when his leg is cut off for fear he will fail to appreciate the extent of his loss. When households cannot increase their consumption, and still more when they must reduce it, the burden on them is lighter if it is less heavily felt. To take money away from people is to interfere with the accepted order of things, and the feeling of loss is acute. To take purchasing power away from people by allowing some measure of inflation is to do what peacetime prosperity always has done, and to conform to existing arrangements to the maximum extent.

Since mild inflation is the appropriate way to conduct defense mobilization, and since mild inflation is just what we are having, what is there to worry about? Why does Government take direct action to keep prices down? Why are we all so heavily taxed? It is sometimes said that Government ought to set up a program providing for price increases of, say, 10% a year, and then let us alone to make our own arrangements on this definite basis. Is this not a good idea?

Moderate inflation according to plan is anything but a good idea, because there can be no such thing. Mild inflation is mild only because we are not sure how much prices will increase over any given month or year, or even that they will increase at all. If we could know that the price level were certain to rise by a definite percentage next year, we should all take immediate steps to protect ourselves against this much of a shrinkage in the purchasing power of money. We should take all the money we had, and all we could borrow, and buy not only goods to store and use up over the coming year, but as much as possible besides to sell later at the higher prices. The obvious consequence would be that prices would rise by a good deal more than 10% almost overnight, and the whole scheme would fail before it had got started.

The way to produce violent inflation is to aim at mild inflation; the way to produce mild inflation is to aim at no inflation. Once the conditions for inflation are present, as they are in the defense economy, Government must make every effort to eliminate the inflationary gap as a whole, and to deal with such specific parts of the total gap as create special complications.

CHAPTER 7

INDIRECT CONTROLS

As GOVERNMENT TAKES the necessary steps to shift resources and build up defense capacity, problems begin to arise on two fronts. On the one hand, the price system proves inadequate to handle the new tasks imposed upon it; on the other hand, attempts to act through existing channels give rise to bottlenecks and inflation. In order to establish a defense economy that will preserve the essential features of peacetime and also be capable of transformation to an effective war economy at short notice, Government must deal with the problems as they arise, exercising both indirect and direct controls over the system.

The distinction between indirect and direct means of control is not always definite, for some measures combine aspects of both. In general, however, we may think of indirect controls as those already existing in the peacetime economy, and of direct controls as being imposed for the purpose of developing the defense economy. Indirect controls thus imply Government action through the price system such as the public has come to accept as part of the business of making a living in peacetime. Direct controls imply Government action that is not customary in peacetime, and that the public supports only because a need for emergency measures is recognized.

In a complete discussion of indirect controls in the peacetime economy, we should have to consider the different ways in which each means of control could be used to achieve different results. Since we are concerned here with only the problems of mobilization, however, we shall treat each of the controls from that standpoint alone.

Money and Credit

A thorough understanding of money and credit, and of the control exercised by Government over them in the United States requires a knowledge of precisely the details that we are going to omit. Readers who are already familiar with the structure and operation of the American banking system may wish to skim over the next few pages quickly, or, if they read more carefully, to supply missing details at the relevant points. Others will get, not a complete picture of money and banking in the United States, but a highly condensed summary of those features that shed most light on Government controls in the defense economy.

In Figure 7.1 we have a model of the American economy showing the most important relationships between firms, households, and the banking system. The area labelled *Member Banks* is supposed to represent the commercial banks that are members of the Federal Reserve System. Out of a total of roughly 15,000 commercial banks, approximately 7,000 are Member Banks, doing about four-fifths of the banking business of the country. The other 8,000 are non-member banks, but through their close relations with Member Banks, they are loosely tied in with the Federal Reserve System.

Commercial banks do a good deal of business with households, and a line connects the two areas in our model. The

Indirect Controls

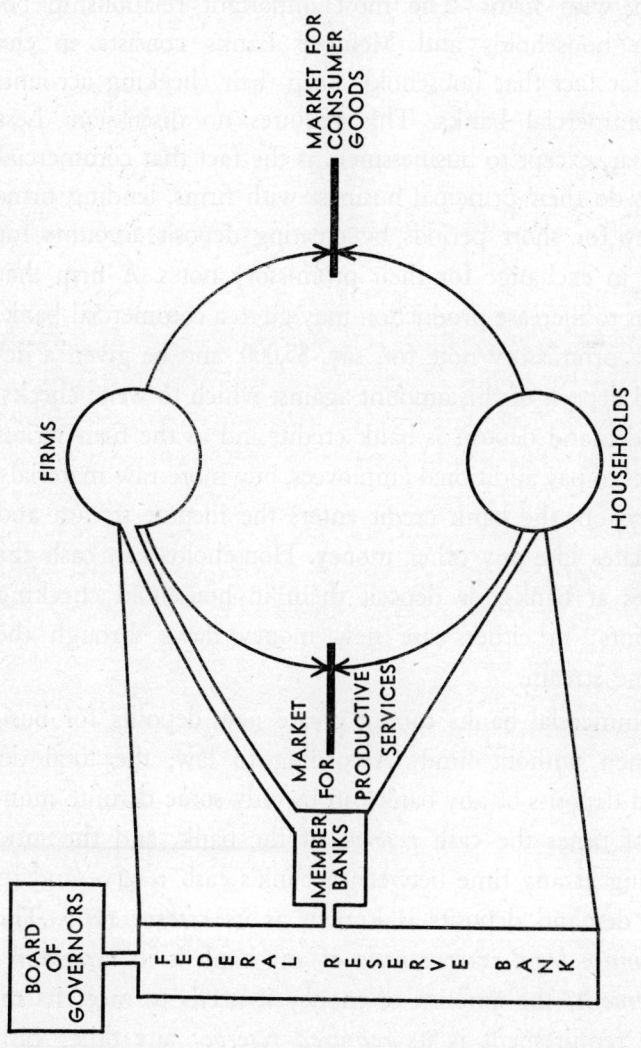

Figure 7.1. THE BANKING SYSTEM

line, however, is not so heavy as that connecting Member Banks with firms. The most important relationship between households and Member Banks consists in the familiar fact that households keep their checking accounts in commercial banks. This requires no discussion. Less familiar, except to businessmen, is the fact that commercial banks do their principal business with firms, lending firms money for short periods by creating deposit accounts for them in exchange for their promissory notes. A firm that wishes to increase production may go to a commercial bank, sign a promissory note for, say, $5,000, and be given a demand deposit of this amount against which to write checks. The demand deposit is bank credit, and as the firm writes checks to pay additional employees, buy more raw materials, and so on, the bank credit enters the income stream and circulates like any other money. Households can cash the checks at banks, or deposit them in household checking accounts; in either case new money flows through the income stream.

Commercial banks cannot create new deposits for businessmen without limit. According to law, the total demand deposits of any bank can be only some definite number of times the cash *reserve* of the bank, and the ratio existing at any time between a bank's cash reserve and its total demand deposits is known as its *reserve ratio*. The *minimum legal reserve ratio* of any bank is its *reserve requirement;* the amount of money it needs to meet its reserve requirement is its *required reserve;* any other cash the bank may have is *excess reserve*. The ability of a commercial bank to create *more bank credit* at any time depends on the *size of its excess reserve;* if it has *no* excess it is "fully loaned up."

Suppose, for example, that a member bank has total demand deposits of $100,000 and cash reserve of $20,000. If its reserve requirement is 20%, the whole $20,000 is required reserve; the bank has no excess reserve; and it can lend by creating demand deposits for firms only as old loans are paid off by previous borrowers. On the other hand, if the same bank had cash reserves of $25,000, it would have $5,000 of excess reserves, and could expand bank credit by increased lending. The particular bank in question could safely lend an amount equal to no more than its excess reserve, since it must be prepared to pay all the checks written on the new deposit at a moment's notice. As such checks were written, however, the people who received them would deposit many of them in their own bank accounts, thus creating some excess reserve for other banks. This sort of transfer of excess reserve from one bank to another has the effect of allowing all the banks combined to lend several times as much as the excess reserves existing at any given time. The important point to note is that the ability of the banking system to lend *more* money at any time depends on the size of the banks' *excess reserves*. The larger the total of excess reserves, the more the banking system can lend by creating new deposit accounts for businessmen.

It now becomes clear that *reserve requirements* greatly affect the ability of banks to create credit. Banks outside the Federal Reserve System have their reserve requirements fixed by state banking laws, but banks within the system have theirs determined by the Board of Governors of the

Federal Reserve System. More important, the Board of Governors has authority to *change* reserve requirements of Member Banks within limits as desired.

Let us look at our model for a moment, and try to clarify the relation of Member Banks to the Federal Reserve System as a whole. The area labelled *Federal Reserve Banks* represents 12 regional bankers' banks located in different sections of the United States. These 12 banks with their branches are owned by the Member Banks, and all the required reserves of Member Banks consist of deposits with the Federal Reserve Banks. As bankers' banks, the Federal Reserve Banks perform the same functions for Member Banks that Member Banks perform for business firms. In other words, the Reserve Banks keep deposits for Member Banks, lend money to them, collect checks for them, and so on, just as Member Banks do these things for businessmen.

At the head of the Federal Reserve System is a group of seven men appointed by the President of the United States, and known as the Board of Governors of the Federal Reserve System. Apart from details, the Board of Governors can be viewed as the agency through which Government acts to control the Member Banks directly, and through them, most of the banks throughout the nation. We are now ready to see how Government may act to control money and credit in the defense economy. The Board of Governors has a number of definite ways of affecting the ability of banks to lend to firms. Since most of the new money that enters the income stream comes from firms that are spending money borrowed from banks, the powers of the Board of Governors are important in any attempt by Government to control inflation. Let us consider the major measures that the Board of Governors may take against inflation, and try to see how effective they are.

1. Within limits, the Board of Governors may *fix the reserve requirements* of Member Banks. Since the excess reserves of banks govern their ability to increase their lending to firms, an *increase* in reserve requirements may restrict lending materially. Any Member Bank with excess reserves must keep a considerable part of the excess on deposit with the Federal Reserve Bank in its district to cover the new higher reserve requirement. Raising reserve requirements thus converts excess reserves into required reserves, and leaves Member Banks with less unused lending power than before.

2. The Board of Governors through an Open Market Committee, may conduct *open market operations*. This means essentially that they may order the Federal Reserve Banks to buy or sell Government Bonds in the open market. By ordering Government Bonds *sold,* the Open Market Committee can reduce the existing reserves of Member Banks. Let us see how this is done.

Federal Reserve Banks always have a large number of Government Bonds in their possession, bought in previous open market operations, or perhaps directly from Government when a new bond issue was made. Looking at our model, we can see that the sale of such bonds by the Federal Reserve Banks *reduces Member Bank reserves.*

Open market sales are made by Federal Reserve Banks to bond dealers, who in turn find buyers for the bonds among banks, insurance companies, and industrial firms that have money to invest. A few households may come into the picture, but we may concentrate our attention on the *firms,* for the effect is similar regardless of the identity of the buyer. In the model, then, let us imagine a block of Government bonds passing from the Federal Reserve Banks to firms as open market selling takes place. The firms pay the Reserve Banks for the bonds by writing checks on their deposits in Member Banks, and the Member Banks must, of course, honor these checks. Since the Federal Reserve Banks hold the deposit accounts that represent the Member Banks' reserves, the Reserve Banks collect from the Member Banks by simply subtracting the amount of the checks from the reserve accounts of the Member Banks. In this way, the open market sale of Government bonds reduces the Member Banks' reserves, and limits the ability of Member Banks to expand credit by increased lending to firms.

3. The Board of Governors *controls the interest rate* that applies to loans made by Federal Reserve Banks to the Member Banks. In order to build up their deposits in the Reserve Banks, and thus get excess reserves on which to base increased lending, Member Banks may borrow from Federal Reserve Banks just as firms borrow from Member Banks. As the interest rate charged on such loans is raised, borrowing becomes more expensive, and Member Banks are discouraged from increasing their reserves in this way. To the extent that Member Banks do continue to borrow, the higher cost will lead them to raise the interest rates that they in turn charge on loans to firms, and credit expansion is restricted.

The three powers of credit control so far considered have, until recently, been the most important means at the disposal of the Board of Governors. When used in combination, they could produce a substantial limiting effect on bank credit expansion, and hence serve to check inflation. By raising reserve requirements the Board of Governors could convert a considerable volume of excess reserves into required reserves. By open market selling, the reserves of Member Banks could be further reduced, thus forcing many banks to borrow at their Reserve Banks to get larger deposit credits. The interest rate on such loans could then be raised, the cost of borrowing increased, and the effect transmitted through the Member Banks and on to businessmen.

Observe, however, that these measures for controlling credit are not very effective if Member Banks have large excess reserves, and if they can easily get more reserves without borrowing from the Reserve Banks. Since World War II Member Banks have been in just this position. During the war, nearly all banks bought very large amounts of newly issued Government bonds, as Government borrowed heavily to pay its expenses not covered by taxes. When Member Banks want more reserves, they can now sell some of the Government bonds they are holding, and deposit the proceeds with the Federal Reserve Banks. Raising reserve requirements and open market selling by the Reserve Banks may thus produce, not borrowing by Member Banks, but open market selling on their own account. In the defense economy this will clearly not do, for the market must not be flooded with old Government bonds at the very time that Government needs to sell large new issues to help in financing mobilization. Furthermore, even if the Board of Governors could make it hard for Member Banks to expand credit, such action would be of doubtful wisdom, for Member Banks must be able to lend money more freely than ever to the firms that are building defense capacity. We conclude, therefore, that what have traditionally been the most powerful means of credit control in peacetime are not well suited for use in checking inflation in the defense economy.

4. The Board of Governors of the Federal Reserve System has authority to *fix the margin requirements* on security trading on the stock exchanges. Suppose the margin requirement is set at 20%. Anyone wishing to buy securities *on margin* may then go to his broker, pay 20% of the value of the securities he wants, and the broker will borrow the other 80% for him at a bank. Raising the margin requirement really means *lowering* the percentage that banks are permitted to *lend* in transactions of this sort. With the margin requirement at 80%, banks can lend only the other 20%; by raising the margin requirement to 100%, the Board of Governors can make securities traders finance all their own buying and selling.

As a device to control inflation, raising margin requirements is not very potent. It tends to keep new money from going into the income stream by forcing security buyers to use their own existing funds rather than bank credit. Sellers of securities thus get money already in circulation instead of money newly created by banks. On the whole, this type of credit control is but a mild check to inflation, and it is important mainly as a step in the desired direction.

5. The Board of Governors can, by special authorization, fix the terms on consumer instalment credit and real estate credit. When households buy such durable consumer goods as automobiles, radios, television sets, ranges, and refrigerators, they usually pay only a percentage of the purchase

price immediately, and pay the balance in a series of monthly instalments that may run on for some time. Similarly, most people who buy homes borrow much of the money on mortgages, and repay their loans over a considerable period of years. By fixing the percentage that must be paid at once, the interest rate charged on the unpaid balance, and the length of time in which payment must be completed, the Board of Governors can produce a significant change in the demand for durable goods and real estate. If people must make larger down payments, carry heavier interest charges, and complete their instalments more quickly, a given amount of spending out of income will buy less than before.

6. A final device for credit control at the disposal of the Board of Governors is requests made to Member Banks to restrict lending for some purposes and increase lending for others. In the peacetime economy, this is usually thought of as a minor type of control, since the Member Banks are not legally bound to follow suggestions thus made to them. On the other hand, individual Member Banks ordinarily like to keep in line with the credit policies of the Reserve System, and by merely stating what is wanted the Board of Governors can accomplish a good deal. This is particularly true in the defense economy, and "voluntary" action under the combined leadership of the Board of Governors and other banking authorities does much to make financing easier for firms engaged in defense production, and more difficult for firms whose expansion would interfere with the mobilization effort.

Summarizing the use of indirect money and credit controls by Government we may say that the traditionally stronger measures of control are less effective in checking inflation than are those that have played a subordinate role in the peacetime economy. In part, this is due to the fact that Member Banks are no longer so dependent on the Federal Reserve Banks for their own credit needs as formerly. More important, however, is the necessity of keeping a large volume of credit available to firms to finance defense production. Even if the Board of Governors could limit the total lending power of Member Banks as effectively as ever, drastic action would hardly be taken for fear of choking off the supply of new funds required for mobilization. On the whole, then, indirect Government control of money and credit appears to make but a modest contribution to the building and operation of the defense economy. Taken by itself, it would be inadequate to accomplish either the shifting of resources or the checking of inflation. We must recognize, however, that no other single set of controls, taken by itself, would be much more impressive. Money and credit control is an essential feature of the defense program. We are used to it and we tend to take it for granted; but we cannot imagine a satisfactory defense economy without it.

Taxation

As we have had occasion to observe in earlier discussions, taxation is one of the most powerful weapons against inflation at the disposal of Government. By levying heavy taxes on both firms and households, Government can draw large amounts of money out of the income stream, thus preventing people from increasing their spending as they otherwise would. Taxes could *conceivably* be increased to the point where all Government expenditure would be financed by taxation, and mobilization would be achieved on a pay-as-you-go basis. Since a good many people believe that this ought to be done, particularly as it appears that inflation would be halted once and for all by the same program, the whole question of taxation in the defense economy is worth careful examination. We shall have to limit ourselves to an overall view, but with the aid of our model we may bring out the most significant points. Let us identify the chief types of taxes that Government may levy, and see what effects they produce on the system.

1. *The Personal Income Tax.* Higher tax rates on individual incomes produce a stronger anti-inflationary effect than almost any other measure that Government can take. The increase in household spending relative to the output of consumer goods could be cut off by taxing increases in income so heavily that households would have no more to spend than before. Personal income taxation has never been carried to this extreme, and there are good reasons why it cannot be in the defense economy. The principal limitation on this sort of taxation is that it is contrary to Government control through the price system. To the extent that Government relies upon changing relative prices of productive services to shift resources, and upon increasing the prices paid for productive services in general to expand their flow to the market, the resulting increases in household income cannot be taxed away as fast as they are earned. This is the really decisive reason why some measure of inflation is practically unavoidable during mobilization. To avoid violent inflation, however, we must act as if it could be prevented altogether, and personal income taxation does help to limit price increases. Moreover, such

taxation can be used to reinforce other Government controls, and can work with the price system rather than in place of it. If households are taxed on the basis of their total incomes as usual, and if no effort is made to tax income increases in particular, higher prices for the labor and resources needed for mobilization will leave the households supplying them materially better off than the rest. It is true that people on relatively fixed incomes, such as college professors and street cleaners, suffer severe cuts in purchasing power. But these people are, on the whole, just the ones who make the smallest direct contributions toward the defense effort, and their losses put pressure on them to take a more active part in the program.

2. *Sales Taxes.* Since households are left after increased income taxes with more money to spend than consumer goods are worth at current prices, Government can follow up the higher income taxes with taxes on the sale of consumer goods and services, thus drawing money out of the income stream as it is spent. Since sales taxes increase the prices that households must pay without increasing the prices that firms receive, such taxes may be judiciously used to direct consumer expenditure into the desired channels. In this respect, oddly enough, the more spectacular sales taxes accomplish little or nothing. Very high "luxury" taxes on such items as fur coats, jewelry, and theater tickets discourage buyers hardly at all. Most of the people who buy such things have high enough incomes to pay for all the consumer goods they want and leave them with large savings besides. When prices are raised by luxury taxes, these people continue to buy what they choose, and merely have a little less income left over to add to their savings.

Despite this fact, high luxury taxes play an important part in any program of sales taxation during mobilization. While they accomplish little in themselves, they do make acceptable the lower taxes on other goods and services that produce positive results. Sales taxes are not popular at best, and tax bills could not even be passed if they provided for higher taxes on necessities than on luxuries and a heavier burden on the poor than on the rich.

What positive results do the more general sales taxes produce? It is often argued that such taxes, instead of checking inflation, actually cause it by directly increasing the prices of consumer goods. Is this so? With the aid of our model the question can be easily answered, but let us first be sure what the question really is. So far, we have been speaking of inflation as a rise in the price level of consumer goods, but in connection with sales taxes there are two of these price levels to consider, and it will not do to get them mixed up.

When we think of the Market for Consumer Goods in our model, we ordinarily suppose that there is only one set of prices in this market, and that the prices paid by households are identical with those received by firms. As soon as sales taxes enter the analysis, this picture changes. What the firms get is no longer what the households pay; the firms get the price to households minus the sales tax. The price level of consumer goods is thus lower to firms than it is to households, and if this fact is kept in mind the effect of sales taxes may be readily seen.

Looking at our model, let us suppose that the price level of consumer goods is raised to households by the imposition of new sales taxes. As households buy goods, the money goes to firms through the market, but the firms must turn over all the sales taxes to Government, thus returning to households as income this much less than the households have spent. On the second round, therefore, consumers have less money to spend than they had at the beginning, and the prices they pay for consumer goods tend to fall. The prices received by firms are thus lower than they were before the sales taxes were levied, and households pay less than the former prices plus the taxes. Sales taxes do not set the inflationary mechanism in motion, for firms are not encouraged to expand their operations, and household income is not increased as a result of the taxes themselves. On the contrary, firms producing the taxed items are discouraged from expanding, for consumers buy less than they otherwise would at the higher prices they must pay.

We may conclude that sales taxes can be called inflationary only if we limit our thinking to the immediate effect of such taxes on the prices that consumers are asked to pay. The less immediate but much more important effect is clearly deflationary, for households earn back their spending minus the taxes on each round. Without increasing earnings from some other source, household income and expenditure would tend to keep shrinking, and a period of general business recession might even be induced.

If the deflationary effect is so unmistakable, why should it be so frequently overlooked? The trouble is mainly that sales taxes are imposed to combat inflation in inflationary periods when the deflationary effects are obscured. In the defense economy, the income stream is naturally fed by mobilization spending, and households may therefore keep on increasing their expenditures despite the imposition of new sales taxes.

3. *Taxes on Production.* Government may levy taxes on the production of goods, and in the defense economy may levy especially high taxes on the production of things that contribute little to the mobilization effort. Taxes on production are similar to sales taxes in their general effects. Firms at first tend to raise their prices enough to cover the whole of the increased taxes they must pay to Government, but the taxes generate no more income for households. Instead, household income tends to be reduced after the first round of spending, and firms find their sales volume declining unless they reduce the prices of consumer goods. Again, the effect is obscured in the defense economy by the increases in income that are taking place in other sectors, but taxes on production are nonetheless deflationary in their overall effects.

4. *Profits Taxes.* Taxes on the profits of firms are raised to high levels in the defense economy for two principal reasons. *First,* as our model shows, profits taxes are a simple device for getting large amounts of money out of the income stream and into the hands of Government, thus helping to check inflation. *Second,* and more important, taxes on profits are a popular type of levy. Most people feel that it is morally wrong for the owners of firms to make large profits from business arising out of a national emergency. It is felt that the managers and employes of corporations may deserve more income, particularly if they are engaged directly in building up defense capacity; but the same cannot be said of the stockholders, who by merely sitting still get larger owners' profits. Hence, some form of *excess*

profits tax has been characteristic of American war economies, and the same type of tax is imposed in the defense economy as well.

The aim of excess profits taxes is to make war or defense production no more profitable than peacetime production, and firms are accordingly taxed at extremely high rates on all profits above previous levels. We need not go into detail concerning the various ways in which excess profits may be defined for tax purposes. It is sufficient to note that the effect though apparently deflationary, is much less deflationary than the large sums of money paid by firms would suggest. For one thing, it is possible that the extra profits, if not taxed, would have been paid out in dividends to owners who would not have spent the money on increased consumption. We have no way of knowing to what extent this would be true, since at best we should be trying to compare what actually happens with what might otherwise have happened, and we have no good basis for such a calculation. A second offsetting effect, though also immeasurable, may be said quite definitely to occur: High excess profits taxes encourage firms to waste the labor and resources of the nation.

What firms waste in the first instance is their owners' money, but what the money pays for is labor and resources that might have found better use during a mobilization effort. Advertising, for instance, is undertaken when it would never justify its cost under ordinary conditions, on the ground that Government pays for most of it, profits after excess profits taxes being little affected. Similarly, efforts to maintain maximum efficiency are relaxed, as high costs mean lower taxes. Salesmen's expense accounts are less closely checked; executives find it desirable to undertake more extensive travel; even wage increases are more readily granted. In brief, high excess profits taxes tend to create a business climate that is anything but favorable to the control of inflation. Whether or not these taxes are still, on balance, deflationary, it is impossible to say. Certainly, businessmen who oppose them have something besides a personal bias to support their claims.

It is difficult to summarize briefly the role of taxation in general in the defence economy, but it may be helpful to bring together some of the conclusions that emerge from our survey. We may say, then, that taxation is Government's most powerful indirect means of controlling inflation. By drawing money out of the income stream, taxation can greatly reduce the excess of consumer spending over the value of consumer goods at current prices. Personal income taxes are strongly deflationary; ordinary profits taxes are also deflationary; but excess profits taxes are deflationary only slightly, if at all. Sales taxes and production taxes are both deflationary in general; they can also be applied to particular commodities to help close specific inflationary gaps and discourage non-essential production.

Inducements to Save

Inflation tends to weaken the ordinary inducements to save by destroying the value of savings. Hence, the strongest inducement to save that Government can provide is the assurance that inflation will not be serious enough to reduce the value of money materially. At this point, however, we get into a circular problem. If people would save enough of their incomes, there would be no inflation to begin with.

If inflation once begins, the incentive to save is already weakened, and with less saving inflation becomes more serious. Since there is to be some inflation in the period of defense mobilization as a whole, Government must try to provide special inducements to save as one means of controlling inflation itself. What special inducements can Government provide?

Any households that reduce their spending on consumer goods are helping to check inflation. If high profits taxes are imposed, the owners of firms will have little more income than ever, and increased personal income taxes may leave them with smaller incomes to spend and save than in the peacetime economy. Salaried employes, similarly, will certainly suffer severe cuts in their spendable incomes. Most of the increased consumer spending that gives rise to serious inflation comes from families whose incomes have been comparatively small, and who can now for the first time afford to buy things they have always wanted. If such people are to be induced to save any large part of their increased incomes, Government must provide them with some powerful incentives.

Unfortunately, the incentives to be provided are more powerful than Government can readily furnish. Experience in World War II gives us the precedents, but experience since then has given savers an education. In World War II, Government issued special bonds, and by means of familiar procedures got households to buy them. War bonds were issued in small denominations, as low as $25.00, and people could buy them for $18.75 for a return of the $25.00 in ten years. The monetary inducement was a higher rate of return than could be obtained by purchasing other comparable securities, and this together with the desire to help pay for the war, was adequate to stimulate a great volume of saving. Arrangements were made for wage earners to buy their bonds by automatic deductions from their weekly pay, and such incentives as "100% of the plant" on payroll deduction were employed to good effect. On the whole, the program was tolerably successful. Why, then, can it not be repeated in the defense economy?

The answer is that inflation has been going on ever since the war bonds were sold, and people who paid $18.75 for a bond have had a chance to discover that the $25.00 they got back would buy less than the $18.75 they paid. The actual return, then, has been less than nothing for many people, and something else will have to be done this time. Government has not yet completed its plans, so we shall waste no space on idle speculation. It is clear, however, that to stimulate increased saving through bond sales, Government must provide some sort of guarantee that buyers will get back more purchasing power than they give up. Higher interest rates may accomplish something. It would also be possible to arrange purchases of defense bonds so as to embody escalator clauses that would provide for returns rising with the cost of living. With only moderate inflation, the cost to Government would be slight, and the saving induced would help to keep inflation from becoming more violent.

Since the relation of saving to inflation is circular, it gives rise to a peculiar danger that is often overlooked. While inflation remains comparatively mild, people may be doing a great deal of saving, and may even save an unusually large part of their total incomes. As evidence to this effect comes to light, we are likely to feel that the new higher rate of saving can be counted upon to reduce the inflationary gap and relieve the upward pressure on prices. Unfortunately, this comforting view of the matter is unsound. When households are accumulating extraordinarily large reserves of cash and other liquid assets, they are not only limiting their current expenditure, but are also building up their capacity to spend in the future. The actual inflationary gap may be negligible at the moment, but the potential gap is growing larger and larger, and the danger of violent inflation is increasing rather than diminishing. If households should become fearful of serious inflation, either because efforts to prevent it were being visibly relaxed or for any other reason, they could spend more of their current incomes and throw their accumulated savings into the market besides.

When Government provides special inducements to save by issuing bonds, the bonds must be attractive not only to buy but also to keep until increased household expenditure is no longer a threat to economic stability.

Production Goals

The last type of indirect control that we shall consider is the fixing of production goals by Government in building defense capacity. In giving defense contracts to firms, Government can specify definite time limits at which output shall have reached a certain level. Or, "targets" may be set up, such as a certain rate of bomber plane production in the whole nation by a particular date. This sort of indirect control may seem too feeble to deserve serious discussion, but it can make a substantial difference to defense mobilization.

Outside industry itself, few people realize how important an incentive the pride of performance is to business executives. In fact, this incentive is at least as powerful as any other single factor in calling forth extraordinary efforts, especially by the management of American corporations. We must remember that most of the top executives in American business get only a small share of the profits made by their firms, and that profits serve as much to measure business performance as to pay the men responsible for it. Business executives are paid more money than most scientists, but both businessmen and scientists work for the approval and respect of their associates as well as for money income.

In the defense economy, high profits taxes and excess profits taxes make profits a less appropriate measure of performance than in peacetime. Moreover, firms building defense capacity on Government contracts may be earning unusually modest returns. If defense mobilization is not to be a source of large profits, the managers of firms must be given some other criterion of superior achievement, and production goals may accomplish what the price system can no longer do automatically.

CHAPTER 8

DIRECT CONTROLS

IN CONTRAST TO INDIRECT controls which function through already existing channels, direct controls require that Government set up special agencies and work out new procedures to direct economic activities. As we have seen, indirect controls as a whole accomplish a great deal, particularly in connection with overall problems like inflation. But controls that work through the price system cannot be relied upon to keep inflation within tolerable limits, and such controls are almost completely ineffective in dealing with bottlenecks that arise from the operation of the price system itself.

Since direct controls are used by Government to supplement indirect measures as the need arises, no detailed account of special agencies and activities would remain valid for long. Not only are new controls continually imposed, but older controls are also modified and relaxed in accordance with changing conditions. To be useful, our treatment of direct controls must be even more general than our earlier discussions, and we must recognize from the beginning that flexibility is a major requirement for the entire program.

Direct Controls and Voluntary Action

Before turning to direct controls as such, we shall do well to clear up some of the confusion that often arises concerning the use of direct measures in contrast to voluntary action. The preservation of individual liberties is generally agreed to be the ultimate goal of the whole mobilization effort, and it is therefore easy to see why people should feel that Government ought to rely on direct controls, if at all, only as a last resort. It is frequently said that Government, instead of ordering people to act, should tell citizens what is needed, and depend on voluntary cooperation to achieve the desired objectives. Thus, to prevent inflation, Government would not go beyond the indirect measures already discussed, but would simply request firms not to raise their prices any higher. Similarly, households would be asked to save more of their incomes, to refrain from increasing their expenditures on consumer goods, and the like. Government does, of course, make such requests as these during mobilization, but the question is why anything more should be done. Is anything wrong with the idea of purely voluntary action, and if so, what?

A good way to see that something is the matter with the idea is to observe that direct action by Government is a result of voluntary action already taken by the American people, who use their Government as the agency through which to act. In other words, citizens of the United States, through their duly elected representatives, have voluntarily chosen to build a defense economy, and Government has been given the powers necessary to get this done. Voluntary action within this program therefore means that people shall be free not to do the things required of them, and that each shall be his own judge of what and how much he will contribute. Suppose that Government were to try checking inflation merely by asking firms not to raise their prices. What would be the result?

To begin with, a good many firms are always about to raise prices to cover recent increases in costs. Under a compulsory Government program, such firms are given special treatment, and their price increases are therefore seen to be justified. If the program were voluntary, however, there would be no responsible public agency to distinguish between those price increases that were justified and those that were not. The least scrupulous would raise prices anyway, and would not only profit at the expense of the rest, but would raise the costs of production of other firms that used their products or had to compete with them for productive services. Firms that were determined not to raise their prices would soon find themselves losing money, and the final reward of virtue would be business failure. Past experience has shown clearly enough how this sort of voluntary action works. It has also shown that those who really want to cooperate are the first to demand that voluntary action be replaced by Government control that will make cooperation effective.

What has been said of firms is just as true of households. Any sort of voluntary action to achieve a common objective requires not that people be left to follow their own inclinations, but that they be organized and directed by agencies of their own choosing. A program of "voluntary credit restraint" by banks, for instance, may restrict lending appreciably just because banks already form a closely knit system. In the defense economy as a whole, the coordinating agencies are branches of Government, and direct controls by Government give effect to the voluntary action of the public. This is the reason why direct controls can be used to only a limited extent. Government will not and can not force the American people into doing more than they think necessary and proper to the mobilization effort.

Price Controls

As a straightforward device for checking inflation, outright price fixing by Government has many apparent advantages. The prices at which firms and households buy and sell can be set at definite levels, and the prices of consumer goods can be held down despite the existence of an inflationary gap.

Government price fixing is so obviously capable of checking inflation that our problem is less to show why this form of direct control is effective than to explain why it is not more so. Let us begin by supposing that Government freezes the prices of all consumer goods at existing levels to halt inflation completely. Can inflation be stopped in this way? The answer is definitely *no*. As long as households want to spend more money on consumer goods than the goods are worth at current prices, there will be some inflation, even if prices are frozen outright. Let us see why.

The price of any consumer good is a certain amount of money exchanged for some definite thing bought by households. To fix prices, then, two controls are necessary: The amounts of money must be fixed; the things changing hands must be kept exactly the same. The first of these controls is comparatively easy to impose and enforce; the second is practically impossible. To take a familiar example, let us consider an automobile the price of which is "fixed" at $2000. The $2000 may stay the same for some time, but the car itself may vary a great deal. The number and quality of accessories, the services performed by the dealer, the terms of sale, guarantee, and literally hundreds of small things add up to the car the buyer gets for his money. As long as households have extra money to spend, Government could hold prices really constant only by undertaking to police every move made in every industry in the country. Firms would steadily reduce the quality of their goods, concentrate on high-priced rather than low-priced lines of merchandise, and develop black-market arrangements for getting money from their buyers in addition to that allowed by the fixed prices of their products. These changes naturally mean a real increase in the price level, though the rise may be hard to measure. Notice, too, that the increase is desired by both buyers and sellers, and that firms are no more "to blame" for the inflation than are households that have the extra money to spend.

Although a general price freeze cannot wholly prevent inflation, it still may appear better than more half-hearted measures of control. This, however, is not true, either; an all-out freeze is hardly as good as no control at all. To freeze all prices at any definite point means to make the price system rigid at the very time when it can function only by being highly flexible. In the peacetime economy, price relationships are constantly changing in response to changing economic conditions. To freeze the price relationships existing at any particular time would produce an endless series of difficulties unless all other economic conditions were also frozen simultaneously. Since defense mobilization involves great and rapid economic changes, it is clear that a price freeze is inconsistent with the main objective, especially as Government wishes to use the price system to the maximum extent. Let us look into the situation a little further.

If the prices of all consumer goods were to be unchanged, Government would have to hold costs down for all firms likewise. If this were not done, mobilization demands would force up labor and resource prices, and the fixed prices of consumer goods would shortly be below production costs. Firms would then have to stop producing, or they would soon fail altogether. Price freezing requires cost freezing, but cost freezing means freezing the incomes of all households, and removing all the usual incentives to shift labor and resources and provide more of both. Without going into the question at length, we can see that what a complete price freeze actually involves is complete Government control over the whole economic system. This is not a defense economy, but is the sort of system that defense mobilization is intended to avoid.

Price control in the defense economy finally reduces to attempts by Government to fix some prices while allowing others to rise, and to change the prices originally fixed as mobilization proceeds. To see how price controls operate let us return to the inflationary gap and the other means of dealing with it.

For the most part, we think of "the" inflationary gap as a general excess of household expenditure over the total value of all consumer goods at existing prices. We have already observed, however, that on closer inspection "the" inflationary gap turns out to be composed of a large number of smaller ones. When households buy consumer goods they do not throw their money into the market at random, but choose specific goods and services out of the available total. When spending on particular items is increasing faster than the flow of these things to the market, individual prices rise though other prices are stable or even falling. Thus, specific inflationary gaps can exist at any time merely because households are concentrating their spending on certain commodities, whether their total spending is increasing or not. If total spending is not increasing relative to the total flow of consumer goods to the market, inflationary gaps in some sectors must be offset by deflationary gaps in others; there is no inflationary gap in the market as a whole. The price system then works out the appropriate shifts in output, income, and the use of resources without extraordinary consequences.

Now, in the defense economy there is an overall inflationary gap, and the small gaps in different sectors of the market do not cancel out. The overall gap may be kept within tolerable limits by indirect controls, especially by taxation. But this is not a complete solution. If a large part of the total gap lies in one or two particular sectors, direct action may be needed at these strategic points. Moreover, the critical regions are subject to change with shifts in output and consumer spending, and gaps may be closed in some sectors only to reappear in others. To take one of the most important examples, let us return to the wage-food-price relationship introduced earlier.

The existence of an overall inflationary gap makes it possible for firms to grant wage increases with confidence that the higher costs can be covered by still higher prices. In other words, small inflationary gaps are present in most sectors of the market. As the households with higher income from wage increases begin to spend more money on food, the small inflationary gap in this sector begins to grow larger. Food production increases very slowly, and the gap persists, with higher food prices raising the cost of living, and leading to further wage increases. Here, then, is a situation in which direct price control would be appropriate. If food prices were to be held down by direct Government order, rises in the cost of living would be substantially checked, and the pressure for further wage increases would be diminished. Similarly, rent control could keep housing prices in line, and with a few other items also controlled, the cost of living might be kept almost stable.

As a hypothetical example of Government price control, food prices serve admirably. As a practical matter, these prices have not been effectively controlled during mobilization, and there is no immediate prospect that they are going to be. The reason for this peculiar state of affairs is that legislation has for some time provided that farm prices be not controlled until they have risen to certain levels relative to other prices. Since food prices on the consumers' side of the market are farm prices on the opposite side, food prices may therefore continue to rise unless other prices are first controlled. But to keep other prices from rising, direct controls would have to be imposed in a great number of sectors in which inflationary gaps are relatively small and the need for direct action controversial. Such thoroughgoing price control is impracticable in the defense economy, at least so long as other measures suffice to prevent violent inflation. Since food prices tend to rise faster than the prices of most other things, the problem may conceivably solve itself as the prices of farm products eventually reach control levels. Meanwhile, mild inflation continues to accompany defense mobilization as we have observed more than once before.

Notice that our conclusion concerning inflation this time as on other occasions applies to the period of mobilization taken as a whole. Shifts in output and expenditure in different sectors of the market must, from time to time, produce price declines that bring controlled items below their permitted ceilings. A generalization that holds good for the total inflationary gap, however, must naturally be valid for its component parts added together. The overall gap and the smaller gaps are not separate things; they are different ways of looking at the same thing.

Before leaving the subject of price control, let us see why it is that when a few prices have once been fixed by Government order, others shortly begin to require attention too. Almost any example that could be taken would bring out the essential point. Let us take the price of sirloin steak.

If Government should fix the price of sirloin steak, permitting no increase in its price while allowing other prices to rise freely, sirloin would soon disappear from the market. Retailers would either sell their sirloin disguised as a different cut of beef, or would grind it into hamburger. Obviously, beef prices in general would have to be controlled; otherwise, the fixed price of sirloin would be a fictitious magnitude with no production and sale taking place. But, if the price of beef alone were held down, farmers would shortly turn to raising sheep or hogs instead, and beef would cease to be produced. So, the prices of substitute meats would have to be controlled also. As soon as this were done, livestock growers could no longer compete with breakfast food manufacturers for corn and oats, and the output of all kinds of meat would shrink. To continue still further, unless the prices of grain other than corn and oats were controlled, farmers would grow mainly the most profitable kinds, and we might wind up with breweries and distilleries having an abundance of grain while people were going without meat.

In the defense economy, direct price control turns out to be a much less promising weapon against inflation than it seems at first sight. Are we to conclude that it is useless? The answer is *no*. Although comparatively feeble in itself, price control plays a vital part in the larger system of controls. If mild inflation is not to become violent, it is essential that speculative opportunities be held to a minimum as prices in general gradually rise. People must not be able to buy given commodities with virtual certainty that they can be sold again at higher prices, or outbursts of spending will produce runaway inflation. The efficacy of price control is not to be judged by the number of prices held in line, nor by the apparent logic of the specific acts of control agencies. The mere fact that everyone knows that Government is quite likely to kill off any good chance to make easy money acts as a powerful brake on inflation.

Wage Controls

The whole problem of inflation would be reduced to much smaller proportions if wage earners did not keep demanding increases in pay. Every time that wages rise, the cost of living is again pushed upward, and wage earners in general are little better off than before. Why do our trade union leaders fail to see this? Why do they keep forcing employers to pay higher wages, when the employes themselves gain nothing, and other people are positively injured? Are union officers ignorant, or indifferent, or what?

These are not profound questions, but they arise often enough to create needless confusion, and we may as well be sure that they are cleared out of our way before going on. We have only to remind ourselves that the concept of "wage earners in general" does not correspond to anything in the American economy to realize that the questions are quite irrelevant. Any single group of employees that gets a wage increase is thereby made better off. If the employes of a single firm or industry get higher wages, their own increased spending will not raise prices perceptibly, and their real incomes as well as their money incomes will rise. If enough other groups are doing the same thing, it is true that none may gain very much. But such gains as are made by any one group depend on its being ahead of the rest. In trying to get in the lead and stay there, a union official is acting in as businesslike and sensible a way as anyone could wish.

Since getting wage increases is a competitive business in which it pays not to get left behind, Government can protect the interests of the public, including wage earners themselves, by imposing wage controls. Anything like a straightforward wage freeze would be inappropriate in the defense economy, for it would be inconsistent with attempts to preserve peacetime arrangements, and to shift labor and resources through the price system. On the other hand, selective wage controls can be used by Government to supplement the price system, and to help break bottlenecks that impede defense mobilization. The goal of wage control in the defense economy is less to hold wages rigidly down than to insure that wage increases work in favor of mobilization instead of against it.

Details aside, Government controls wages by requiring employers to submit proposed wage increases to a Government agency for approval. As the cost of living rises, wages must be raised for those employes covered by escalator clauses in union contracts, and employes not so covered tend to demand at least equal treatment. By allowing wages to be raised more rapidly by firms engaged in defense production than by other firms competing for the same labor and resources, Government can eliminate many bottlenecks that would otherwise develop. Since civilian producers who cannot offer wages comparable to those paid in defense industries lose employes, they reduce output and free scarce raw materials for defense production. Selective wage control is therefore a powerful means of shifting resources as well as labor from non-essential to essential uses.

Although wages in general keep rising, the rise is at a slower rate than it would be without control. The process of getting increases approved by Government is time consuming; the increases granted are frequently smaller than those proposed; and the discrimination against civilian producers holds wages down substantially in non-essential industries. As a result, the competitive pressure for wage increases is partially relieved, and inflation is retarded.

Priorities and Allocations

In discussing direct controls we have been moving from the less to the more positive devices. If price and wage controls do not operate through the price system they at least operate on it, leaving firms and households to respond to the changes introduced. Priorities and allocations short-circuit the price system altogether, functioning not by producing price effects but by controlling physical quantities of resources. Let us discuss these two devices in order.

1. *Priorities*. Government sets up a system of priorities to break production bottlenecks, withhold strategic resources from non-essential uses, and channel scarce materials into defense production. Omitting details, we may say briefly that a priorities system works as follows:

Producers of essential materials, such as steel, copper, and tin, fill orders from other firms in accordance with priority ratings issued by Government. By assigning these ratings in accordance with the needs of the defense program, Government can cut off the competition of non-essential producers, even if they have more money to spend than defense industries.

A system of priorities is hard to administer for two reasons. In the first place, all firms wanting essential materials press their claims on Government, with the result that the highest priorities tend to be given too freely, and even in excess of the materials to be had. In the second place, Government must coordinate its different priorities in order to be sure that enough of all the materials needed for defense production reaches selected firms. A contractor, for instance, may have high priorities on most of the materials needed to build a defense plant, and for want of some minor item may be unable to finish the job. All the resources committed to the plant are therefore going to waste. Similarly, there is no point in insuring that firms get all their needed materials, if the necessary labor is not also available.

Despite these difficulties, a priorities system is an important feature of the defense economy, and mobilization would be less successful without it.

2. *Allocations.* Under a priorities system, the favored firms are given the *right* to have their orders filled in preference to those of other firms. Government, however, leaves it to the firms with high priorities to go out and find the materials they need, and there is no assurance that this can always be done. A system of allocations can be thought of as an attempt to go the rest of the way by guaranteeing that defense industries will get what they require.

Under a priorities system, Government controls the *demand* for strategic materials; under an allocation system, it controls the *supply*. In allocating materials, Government estimates the total amounts that will be available, and then apportions the total among various uses in order of urgency. The firms pay for what they get, and Government need not actually handle any of the materials, merely telling their possessors how much to sell and to whom.

Priorities and allocations combined give Government control of both demand and supply, and short-cut the price system completely. With price controls also in effect, part of the economy functions much like a socialist system. In the defense economy, priorities, allocations, and price control are carried only far enough to break bottlenecks and prevent new ones from developing as mobilization proceeds. The cooperation of firms is obviously essential, and Government tends to act on a limited scale.

Rationing

Rationing is a device for controlling demand, and is thus comparable to a system of priorities. Ordinarily, however, rationing is thought of as a device for controlling the demand of consumers alone, though the term is sometimes applied to money and credit. Let us begin with consumer rationing.

1. Rationing of consumer goods is effected by the price system in the peacetime economy. As prices are higher or lower, fewer or more households are able and willing to buy particular goods. If prices are to be fixed by Government, instead of by the action of demand and supply in the market, the goods whose prices are held down must be rationed in some special way. If the price of any good is lower than households are prepared to pay, there will be an excess demand for the good. In the peacetime economy, such an excess demand is soon met by a higher price or an increase in production or both, but in the defense economy neither of these reactions is likely to follow. Prices are controlled, as a rule, just because they would otherwise rise rapidly, and because the output of consumer goods cannot be increased very much during mobilization.

If the prices of consumer goods are being held below what households are able and willing to pay, it is clear that the total flow of goods to the market is smaller than households are prepared to take. The result, then, must be that the households who get there first will get what there is, and the rest will get nothing. In these circumstances, people will leave their work to stand in line half the day, waiting to buy what they want, and much time and energy will be spent to no good purpose. Rationing by Government meets the situation by cutting off excess consumer demand, and insuring that all households will get a fair chance to buy scarce goods.

To ration consumer goods, Government first estimates the total flows of scarce items that will be coming to the market, and then issues coupons to households, entitling buyers to purchase limited quantities in rough accordance with need. As consumers buy the rationed items from retailers, coupons as well as money change hands, and people who would pay far more than the controlled prices get no more goods than the rest.

At this point, the *black market* begins to develop. In contrast to purchase and sale under Government control, the black market is the free market of peacetime trying to function despite mobilization conditions. In the defense economy, households have more money to spend than would buy the whole output of consumer goods at controlled prices. In order to get more goods than they are allowed under Government rationing, consumers are therefore prepared to pay more than the "ceiling" prices in effect, and sellers are strongly tempted to evade Government regulations. If special deals begin to be made on any considerable scale, the whole system of price control is endangered. The chief incentive that consumers have to put up with Government interference is the conviction that they are making some contribution to the mobilization effort. If many consumers discover that their own sacrifices are mainly contributing to the well-being of their less scrupulous fellows, the cooperation necessary to successful rationing must vanish, and black market arrangements dominate the scene. Since Government cannot put most of the people in the country in jail for evasion, it is necessary to keep black markets from growing up from the outset. How can this be done?

The most effective device that Government can employ is to make supplies to retailers dependent on the coupons they turn in to wholesalers, supplies to wholesalers dependent on coupons turned in to jobbers or manufacturers, and so on. If rationing is controlled in this way, comparatively few outside deals can be profitably made, for failure to collect coupons at any stage in the distributing process means that the seller cannot continue to get goods. Evasion is, of course, still possible, but it takes on a flavor of racketeering that makes it much easier for Government to identify lawbreakers and deal harshly with them.

Rationing by Government coupon is unnecessary when flows of goods are adequate, and when prices are not held down by controls. Even when goods are scarce and prices controlled, a few items such as cigarettes may be rationed by manufacturers themselves instead of by Government. Such exceptions exist if the manufacturers are large firms that control closely the distribution of their products throughout the country, for such firms can prevent black markets in their products, and they will lose goodwill and prestige if they do not. At the other extreme, effective rationing is virtually impossible where channels of distribution are not well organized, and where many small firms may be producing and selling directly to consumers. If several thousand farmers are each raising and slaughtering a few meat animals, Government can hardly prevent their selling small amounts of meat to people who drive out to the farms. Although rationing cannot be made air tight, it can nevertheless be a tolerably effective substitute for the price system in distributing price-controlled consumer goods.

Before leaving the question of rationing, we should notice a limitation that is particularly applicable to the defense economy. Rationing, more than most other Government direct controls, requires active cooperation on the part of the public. In an all-out war economy, evasion is mostly confined to unpatriotic people, and social disapproval tends to keep them from wrecking the system. In the defense economy, people have less incentive to conform to unpleasant regulations, and black markets tend to develop on a larger scale. If Government tries to impose more restrictions than are clearly necessary, the system of controls, instead of preparing the economy for war, breaks down before the gravest emergency even arises. Since effective price control necessarily involves a good deal of consumer rationing, Government must move cautiously in the use of both these direct measures of guiding economic activity.

2. *Credit Rationing.* In our discussion of indirect controls over money and credit we observed that the Board of Governors of the Federal Reserve System can enlist the aid of commercial banks in limiting the expansion of loans to non-essential industry, and making credit freely available to defense producers. This indirect action may be reinforced by direct Government rationing of credit as the need develops. Like other forms of rationing, credit rationing controls the demand rather than the supply. Since the banks can always be given increased lending power by ordinary peacetime methods, there is no danger of there being too little bank credit to go around. The object of credit rationing is to cut off the credit demands of non-

essential producers to keep them from competing for scarce labor and materials.

Outright credit rationing by Government plays a minor role in the defense economy, for it accomplishes little that cannot more easily be done through priorities and allocations. Instead of requiring that banks make only approved loans, Government may keep resources out of the hands of non-essential producers, and thus keep their demand for loans from even arising.

Although for the most part Government need not concern itself in any new way with the supply of credit, there is one point at which direct action may be taken. Firms with defense contracts will usually find it easy enough to borrow from banks, but firms that are likely to be given defense contracts in the future may have no immediate prospects on which to base requests for loans. Some of these firms may be steadily losing money in civilian production, and in the peacetime economy would fail without causing much concern. In the defense economy, however, their facilities may be badly needed, and Government action is required to keep them alive. The solution is direct Government lending through an agency like the Reconstruction Finance Corporation. These loans are not always wisely made, and some firms with little claim to preference may be favored. Even with the greatest care, Government cannot guarantee that any given loan will be worthwhile, for the future is too uncertain. The uncertainty, however, is the justification for direct Government lending as a whole, and despite imperfections in practice, the program is an important part of the mobilization effort.

Government Ownership

Government ownership and operation of industry is obviously the highest degree of direct control over the economy. Since defense mobilization is not designed to convert the nation to socialism, this form of control is limited to two small but critical sectors of the system.

1. Government acquires and operates defense plants of special types, of which atomic and hydrogen bomb installations are examples. In general, we may say that Government ownership is limited to projects requiring secrecy, highly specialized equipment, and the expenditure of great sums of money. In other words, the projects must be closely supervised by Government in any event, and they would be beyond the financial resources of most private firms, as well as largely useless to them in the peacetime economy. Some exceptions to these generalizations must be admitted, for Government may short circuit all less extreme devices in the face of particular emergencies in order to preserve the national security.

2. Government may take over private firms or industries if quick action is needed to prevent interruptions in output from delaying mobilization. The standard example of this type of control is the temporary seizure by Government of firms in which disputes between labor and management cannot be quickly resolved, and production falls off or threatens to stop entirely. By taking over such firms, Government can impose military regulations on both labor and management, and force them to maintain production pending settlement of their differences.

When Government takes over a firm, the act is mainly symbolic. An executive order issued by the President of the

United States is transmitted to the management of the firm, and Government thereby "takes possession." The day to day business of the firm continues as usual, with the same people doing their usual work, and with any profits made going to the regular stockholders instead of the new "owner." Even if the Army "moves into a plant," the act is likely to be nearly invisible. A full-fledged General may occupy one of the offices, and some men in uniform may be seen here and there, but everything goes on about as before.

Of course, the fact that Government seizure involves no extraordinary changes in the operations of a firm is precisely what makes it effective. Government takes over on purpose to preserve existing conditions when they would otherwise have been disrupted. A telegram or a few men in uniform may be the only tangible evidence that the sovereign power of Government is on the scene, but everything is in principle quite different. Management and wage earners alike have ceased to be free agents, and have acquired a status comparable to that enjoyed by members of the armed forces. Government may issue few orders, but those it does issue must be obeyed, and this is understood by everyone concerned from the outset.

The seizure of private firms is one of the least spectacular yet one of the most extreme measures of direct control Government can invoke. The summary imprisonment or execution of citizens involves hardly more exercise of arbitrary power. Except in great emergencies, Government seizure is unlikely to be attempted. If it is attempted in other circumstances, firms may appeal to the courts with some confidence that Government will be forced to withdraw.

Chapter 9

CONCLUSION

The great experiment of defense mobilization has not yet met its ultimate test, and we have no way of knowing what the final outcome of our efforts will be. Although the decisive test of the adequacy of our preparations can only be an all-out war, it is just this ordeal that we hope to avoid. Meanwhile, less crucial tests of our abilities are continually being made as the problems of mobilization emerge and are dealt with one by one. Since we can foresee these problems, and since we know what to do about them, we may be sure that we are not attempting the impossible. Substantial progress has indeed been made already, and impressive successes are being achieved every day.

As our doubts about the feasibility of defense mobilization subside, we are finding other things to worry about. We worry, of course, about the danger of all-out war, but everyone knows too well what it means to feel much like talking about it. Many of us are starting to look ahead to the day when our major mobilization effort will have been completed, and only comparatively small additions to defense capacity will continue to be made. If and when inflationary pressures subside, will we experience a collapse of income and employment such as we have had in major peacetime depressions? If war fails to materialize, can we run our defense economy indefinitely without disaster?

Having raised this question, we should doubtless make

some attempt to answer it. The only honest answer, however, is that nobody knows. If all the conditions we shall have to face could be precisely specified, economic analysis could give us the solution. As it is, we must wait and see. In the course of time we shall have the facts we need, and it is to be hoped that the reader has acquired a technique that will enable him to analyze future developments as they occur.

In place of any attempt at prediction, we may close our discussion with something less futile. This book has been called a primer because it is intended to be an introduction to its subject. It is, moreover, an analytical introduction in the sense that descriptive details have been deliberately excluded in order to keep them from obscuring the main issues. Once the broader aspects of the subject have been analyzed, the details very readily fall into place, becoming both more intelligible and more interesting.

The following books are recommended to users of this small volume who wish to read somewhat further in one direction or another:

1. All introductory economics textbooks give most of their space to the peacetime economy. Among the dozens of good general texts, P. A. Samuelson, *Economics, An Introductory Analysis* (McGraw-Hill, 1951), is by all odds the most readable. L. V. Chandler, *A Preface to Economics* (Harper, 1947), is a short and excellent survey. R. V. Clemence, *Income Analysis* (Addison-Wesley, 1951), develops the model technique with more technical refinements than were suitable to the present work. S. H. Slichter, *The American Economy, Its Problems and Prospects* (Knopf, 1948), is adequately described by its title.

Conclusion

With the exception of Professor Samuelson's textbook, all the books in this group are small volumes that can be read through in a few hours.

2. Two of the best books on the war economy, are likewise two of the smallest. A. C. Pigou, *The Political Economy of War* (Macmillan, 1940), and L. Robbins, *The Economic Problem in Peace and War* (Macmillan, 1947), are by eminent British economists.

3. Most books on the defense economy are of substantial size, and contain a good deal of historical background and descriptive matter. A number of them deal not only with problems of mobilization, but also with those of war. W. G. Campbell & Others, *Economics of Mobilization and War* (Irwin, 1952), is obviously one of these; six authors contribute chapters on their specialties, supplying much detail not included in the present volume. J. Backman & Others, *War and Defense Economics* (Rinehart, 1952), is a larger book of the same sort, six chapters of which have been published separately in J. Backman, *The Economics of Armament Inflation* (1951). S. E. Harris, *The Economics of Mobilization and Inflation* (Norton, 1951), is rather more analytical than the others. Any of them, however, would be a good sequel to this book.

On a somewhat higher technical level L. V. Chandler & D. H. Wallace, *Economic Mobilization and Stabilization* (Holt, 1951), is a collection of twenty-six articles, most of them reprinted from economic journals and similar sources. The volume contains a good selected bibliography. Lincoln, Stone, & Harvey, *Economics of National Security* (Prentice-Hall, 1950), is especially strong on facts and figures.

4. Special aspects of mobilization are dealt with by a

number of books. A. G. Hart and E. C. Brown, *Financing Defense* (Twentieth Century Fund, 1951) is concerned with Federal taxing and spending. L. V. Chandler, *Inflation in the United States, 1940-1948* (Harper, 1951), is a good combination of history, statistics, and economic analysis. A. G. Hart, *Defense Without Inflation* (Twentieth Century Fund, 1951), is a companion volume to *Financing Defense*. "Defense without inflation" appears to be a contradiction in terms, but Professor Hart's book is in closer touch with reality than the title would suggest.

5. Money and credit controls are discussed in Professor Samuelson's textbook as well as in many others. One of the best things in print on the subject continues to be *The Federal Reserve System, Its Purposes and Functions,* a booklet available without charge from The Board of Governors of the Federal Reserve System, Washington, D. C.

6. The future may be said to be anybody's guess, but not in the sense that one man's guess is quite as interesting as another's. The guesses of an able economist who has been doing well at the game for some time are worth some attention, especially if the economist is Professor Slichter who knows when he is guessing and when he is not. S. H. Slichter, *What's Ahead for American Business* (Little, Brown, 1951), does in two-hundred small pages what some readers may have been looking for in our final chapter. Perhaps a reference to his book will be an appropriate conclusion to this one.